REAL MESSAGES FROM
HEAVEN 2

DESTINY IMAGE BOOKS BY FAYE ALDRIDGE

Real Messages From Heaven

REAL MESSAGES FROM
HEAVEN 2

True Stories of Miracles and
Divine Interventions That Offer Proof of
Life After Death

FAYE ALDRIDGE

DESTINY IMAGE® PUBLISHERS, INC.

P.O. Box 310, Shippensburg, PA 17257-0310

"Promoting Inspired Lives."

This book and all other Destiny Image, Revival Press, MercyPlace, Fresh Bread, Destiny Image Fiction, and Treasure House books are available at Christian bookstores and distributors worldwide.

For a U.S. bookstore nearest you, call **1-800-722-6774**.

For more information on foreign distributors, call **717-532-3040**.

Reach us on the Internet: **www.destinyimage.com**.

ISBN 13 TP: 978-0-7684-0324-4

ISBN 13 Ebook: 978-0-7684-8576-9

For Worldwide Distribution, Printed in the U.S.A.

1 2 3 4 5 6 7 8 / 17 16 15 14 13

ACKNOWLEDGMENT

I sincerely offer my thanks to all of the wonderful people who allowed me to tell their amazing stories in the following pages. Retelling each story is a way of offering praise to God for allowing us to see His blessed hope in every phase and circumstance of our lives. These touching stories remind us that death is the end here and the beginning there, in Heaven or hell. I am blessed to be able to tell these true stories that give us the opportunity to pause, reflect, and take stock of our lives. We are not without hope. Jesus Christ is our hope! While there is life, there is still time to make the decision to accept Jesus as Savior. That decision assures each of us a place in Heaven for eternity!

CONTENTS

INTRODUCTION

While compiling this book and interviewing people who have lived, died, and returned to tell what happened, I realized how blessed I am to be a storyteller. My words on paper cannot convey the emotion I feel when I am with a person who has traveled from earth to Heaven to earth. People who have traveled beyond this world have an uncommon sparkle in their eyes. I always sense an undertone of excitement and anticipation in their voices that is unmistakable!

I never tire of hearing extraordinary accounts of visits from loved ones who have died and returned from Heaven in spirit to this place to convey a message of hope or comfort to one who grieves. After-death appearances, near-death experiences, and angel appearances are nothing new biblically speaking. Each encounter is a gift from God to be revered and shared.

In the following pages, you will read about Josie Mitchell, a Muscogee Creek-Seminole Indian, who lived through the terrorist bombing of the Alfred P. Murrah Federal Building in Oklahoma City in 1995. He had some help from an *angel!*

Nancy Strickland-Fields, a *Lumbee* Indian, experienced a truly remarkable *holy encounter with God* in Pembroke, North Carolina, just hours after her mother died. That glimpse of eternity changed her life!

John Crawford, a land surveyor from California, died from a heart attack. He shared details of a *near-death* experience. Suddenly, he found himself out of his body traveling toward a bright band of silver and gold lights. The lights shimmered in the darkening twilight far off in the western horizon of the Pacific Ocean!

Justin Cheatham was a soldier in Iraq when a deceased loved one paid him an *after-death* visit and foretold of a significant event in his future. The same deceased loved one made a second visit that night, to someone on another continent!

Angel appearances are common occurrences having been documented all through the Bible. In the 18th chapter of Genesis, angels in the form of humans appeared to Abraham and announced the birth of Isaac to Abraham and Sarah in their old age. Psalms 34:7 reminds us, *"The angel of the Lord encamps around those who fear Him, and rescues them."* God sends His angels to help us.

In the Bible in Second Corinthians 12, Saint Paul tells of his own journey beyond this life.

> *I know a man in Christ who fourteen years ago—whether in the body I do not know, or out of the body I do not know, God knows—such a man was caught up to the third heaven. And I know how such a man...was caught up into Paradise and heard inexpressible words, which a man is not permitted to speak* (2 Corinthians 12:2-4).

Paul was describing his own vision and revelation. He could not fully explain what happened, yet his explanation made it clear that he traveled beyond this earthly realm. That sounds similar to how some describe their near-death experiences.

The Bible tells of an after-death appearance in the 17th chapter of Matthew. The Scripture tells us that Jesus took with Him Peter, James, and John, three of His disciples, up to a high mountain by themselves.

Furthermore, beginning in the second verse, we learn that *"He (Jesus) was transfigured before them; and His face shone like the sun, and His garment became as white as light"* (Matt. 17:2). Moses and Elijah, who had been dead for hundreds of years, appeared to them there, talking to Jesus. All three disciples witnessed the after-death appearances of Moses and Elijah before they vanished from sight! In John 8:51, Jesus said, *"Truly, truly, I say to you, if anyone keeps My word he will never see death."*

The stories you are about to read are all positive experiences. That does not mean that all after-death experiences are positive. Clearly, the absence of "to hell and back stories" in this book should not be misinterpreted. I found no one willing to tell me his or her stories about hell. One chapter does address hell experiences as told to other authors. Most people are not willing to share "to hell and back" experiences because they are unpleasant and those chilling accounts remain closeted. There is a vast difference between the after-death experience of the saved Christian and the lost non-Christian.

Matthew 7:13-14 refers to Heaven and hell.

> *Enter by the narrow gate; for the gate is wide and the way is broad that leads to destruction, and there are many who enter through it. For the gate is small and the way is narrow that leads to life, and there are few who find it.*

Dr. Maurice Rawlings, a well-known cardiologist, has communicated with numerous patients who died and went to hell. By modern methods, those patients lived after resuscitation. Some of his patients were willing to describe frightening hellish encounters in the minutes immediately following their resuscitation. Dr. Rawlings documented many of their life-changing experiences in his book titled, *To Hell and Back*. I encourage others to read his enlightening messages. I strongly believe we should be aware of the fact that not all go to Heaven. Heaven and hell are real places. Our individual decision to accept Jesus or to reject Him determines where we will spend eternity. We will spend eternity in either Heaven or hell; there is nothing else.

Chapter 1

ANGEL IN OKLAHOMA CITY

On April 19, 1995, a terrorist bomb attack on the Alfred P. Murrah Federal Building in downtown Oklahoma City happened at 9:02 in the morning. It was a hazy day, having rained the day before, and rain was in the forecast for the next day.[1] Jacqualine Mitchell worked near the Will Rogers World Airport, about ten miles away, and she heard the explosion. She initially thought a plane crashed at the airport.

Jacqualine had no idea that her dad and stepmother had gone to the Social Security Office at the Federal Building that morning. She was shocked when she heard reports that the bombing had turned the area into a scene resembling a war-torn third world country. The deafening, earth-shaking explosion blew windows out from the structure while walls and ceilings came crashing down. Concrete reinforced floors collapsed, falling on top of each other, reducing the front of the building to an enormous pile of debris and rubble. Cars burned in the surrounding parking lots. Smoke plumes rose as hysteria sent bystanders running for cover in every direction.

In front of the building, shattered glass, pieces of sheetrock, concrete, metal cables, and debris spilled forth, mounding up to two stories high and spilling over onto the adjacent street and parking lot. Frightened, confused, and bloody survivors poured out of the stairwells of the building. The structure was nine stories tall. A hundred and sixty-eight adults and children died from the devastation. A childcare center was located on the second floor just thirty feet from the explosion. Only six children survived the bombing. The explosion injured more than 680 people that day. The explosion was massive, demolishing the Alfred P. Murrah Federal Building and destroying or damaging 324 buildings over a sixteen-block area![2]

Josie Mitchell, accompanied by his wife, Leigh, left home that morning, heading for the Alfred P. Murrah Federal Building. Josie had business to attend to at the Social Security Office on the first floor of the Federal Building. The couple waited in the reception area for a few minutes before an employee called Josie's name. Leigh remained in the waiting area near the front of the building when Josie proceeded to an office closer to the rear of the building with the Social Security employee.

Mr. Mitchell needed additional information he had left with his wife and he was in a hallway walking toward the front of the building when the explosion occurred. The horrific explosion plunged Mr. Mitchell into pitch-black darkness. Thick dust, vapors and debris filled the air, making it nearly impossible to breathe. Walls and ceilings collapsed, crashing down, burying many of the people who did and did not survive in the rubble.

Mr. Mitchell found himself lying dazed in the rubble, bleeding, hurting, disoriented, and nearly deaf. The shock wave from the explosion injured his eardrums, leaving him with a deafening ringing sound in his ears. He felt blood trickling from his head and something hit him in the right eye. Mr. Mitchell's ability to hear and see was diminished instantly. He could see nothing around him.

Mr. Mitchell landed in a small space beneath one wall that collapsed, leaning against another section of wall. The fact that he was in a hallway was a blessing, because one wall supported a portion of the falling wall and kept it from crushing him. Mr. Mitchell struggled to breathe in the thick dust. Electrical wires dangled from overhead. He felt his surroundings there in the darkness but he did not know what he could safely touch. Mr. Mitchell could not imagine how he would get out of the pile of rubble that enclosed him.

Suddenly Mr. Mitchell saw a woman dressed in dazzling white standing near him. In his confusion, he thought it was Leigh. The woman called him by name and Josie was able to hear her plainly in spite of the persistent ringing in his ears.

She said, "How are you Joe?"

Josie replied, "Doing all right, how about you?"

The woman continued talking, saying, "If you will follow me, I will get you out of here." The woman dressed in white did not walk ahead of Mr. Mitchell; *she floated ahead of him* as she took the lead.

Mr. Mitchell focused on the white dress in the darkness and he crawled after the woman with great difficulty. He attempted to slow the woman down by saying to her, "You better be careful in all of this debris. You can't see where you are going and you could get hurt." He struggled but managed to keep up.

In a few minutes, Mr. Mitchell saw a ray of light ahead of him and he concentrated on making his way toward the source of the light. Strangely, the woman disappeared at that time. He reached a door located in the rear of the building that was slightly ajar and he wobbled through the door and emerged into the arms of a rescuer.

The first thing Mr. Mitchell asked his rescuer was the whereabouts of the woman in the white dress. The man assured him that no one came out of that door ahead of him. The worker who led Mr. Mitchell to triage assured him he would have seen anyone who exited there.

In the following days, Mr. Mitchell learned his wife did not survive the blast. The initial explosion killed her and workers discovered her body days later. The whole world changed that day for Josie Mitchell, but he did survive to tell the story about the angel that God sent him that saved his life.

In the days that followed that terrible event, numerous people questioned Josie about his miraculous survival. He was quick to share his faith and to give God all the glory for protecting him and for sending an angel that helped him escape.

Mr. Mitchell told family members, "I don't know why God spared me, but I know He did spare me for a reason. I am trying to find my way back to see what it is that He wants me to do."

Mr. Mitchell entered full-time ministry and shared his testimony on numerous occasions until the time of his death in 2007. His family members speak lovingly of him. They remember Josie as being funny, outspoken, and a wonderful man of God with a deep desire to share his steadfast faith with others.

Notes

1. http://www.the-office.com/okc

2. wikipedia.org/wiki/Oklahoma

Chapter 2

HOLY ENCOUNTER IN PEMBROKE, NORTH CAROLINA

PART 1

Eartle Jane Strickland was a *Lumbee* Indian, born in June of 1934 in Robeson County, North Carolina. One day from her childhood stood out from all the rest. Her mother approached her quietly one morning and asked if she would like to accompany her on a trip to town. That day was the first day the mother and daughter had ever spent time together without all of the other children around.

Eartle was only six years old and she was very excited to get to go into the town of Lumberton. Serious segregation (Jim Crow Laws applied to Indians in Lumberton) existed in that town in those days. The public drinking fountains, bathrooms, and entrances were marked with signs that clearly divided people into three separate categories, white, black, and red, segregating all three races in public places.

Eartle and her mom's skin was fairer than most *Lumbee* Indians. For that reason, no one questioned them when they entered the drugstore that day and ordered a cherry coke to share. Later they shopped for fabric to make all five girls new dresses, and Eartle helped her mom choose the material.

The two of them returned home later and Eartle smiled broadly when the other children teased her about being so special and going into the drugstore. The drugstore did not knowingly permit Indians to enter. The day would stay in Eartle's mind as a freeze frame for all her years to come. The time she spent with her mom that day was one the best times of her life!

It was customary for her mother, Lillian Oxendine, to gather her children around her feet each night and read the Bible to them before bedtime. That night was no different. The children drew near their mother and eagerly listened while she read to them. Their mother's nearly floor length hair was loose that night and the children draped her long tresses over their heads having childish fun. Lillian said her head was hurting badly so she took down her bun hoping to ease the pain.

Without any warning, Lillian died in her sleep that night in the early morning hours of May 6, 1941. Her family buried her in the family cemetery near their home. They mourned Lillian's death and her children never forgot their mother's tender love and kindness.

PART 2

The night of May 6, 1996, was one of the nights when Eartle stayed in the home of her sister, Emma, in Pembroke, North Carolina. She had been staying with her sister for the three previous months due to serious health concerns. Eartle suffered from severe congestive heart failure, diabetes, and kidney failure and she had been very ill. That particular night, Eartle felt unusually good and the two sisters laughed, joked, and reminisced about their childhood and fond memories of their mother, whom they had not made mention of in decades.

Like her mother, without warning, Eartle passed away that night in her sleep during the early morning hours, just as her mother did and just a day after the anniversary date of her mother's death. Emma went to awaken Eartle the next morning and could hardly believe it when she realized her sister had passed away.

Nancy Strickland Fields, Eartle's daughter, received the news later that morning after she went to work in Charlotte, North Carolina. Charlotte was a little over a hundred miles from Pembroke, where her mother was staying with Emma.

Nancy and Eartle shared a very close and loving relationship. There was an extra special mother-daughter bond between the two of them. Eartle had helped Nancy raise her daughter, Kierra. The news devastated Nancy. Nancy and her friend, Stacy, drove to Pembroke later that afternoon.

That night, darkness and sadness settled over that home in the country like a heavy veil. As Nancy and her Aunt Emma gathered clothing and other things to take to the funeral home, Nancy decided she wanted to bury her mother with her mother's ring and her wedding ring. While Emma and Eartle were talking the night before, Emma noticed that Eartle had taken the rings off. That was her routine after her evening round of dialysis because her fingers had a tendency to swell. Nancy and Emma began looking around the room for the rings.

The futile search for the rings and the reality of her mother's death overwhelmed Nancy. She sat in a chair in the bedroom where her mom had died, looking through a small basket of her mom's personal belongings, thinking perhaps she had put the rings in there. The rings seemed to have disappeared. Nancy took a deep breath and glanced up toward a window that faced the front of the house. She noticed a brilliant shining light the size of a silver dollar gently hovering in the lower left-hand corner of the window.

The unusual light immediately caught Nancy's attention. At first she thought it was from an approaching car, perhaps a flashlight, or a reflection from something inside the house, but that was not the case. Close inspection revealed it was a light within itself. The shimmering white light moved slowly to the center of the window where it continued to hover slightly, as if alive. At that moment, Nancy felt a touch on the top of her head that ran from the front of her hairline to the back of her head. It reminded her of how her mom used to part her hair with her long fingernail before she braided it when she was a little girl. In that motion, she felt her soul open up. It felt like God had lifted a pitcher over her head filled with peace and was pouring it into her body.

Nancy experienced holy, warm, otherworldly peace flowing into her body through the top of her head, moving slowly downward through her neck and shoulders. It was an extremely intense feeling—but at the same time the most calming, comforting sensation she had ever known and words seem to be inadequate when describing it.

Nancy was exhilarated! When the extraordinary peace filled her chest, she experienced a powerful rapid-fire question and answer session permeating her being as if God in Heaven was telling her answers to all of creation. As the feeling intensified and slowly moved through her body, she instantly received some profound knowledge. She heard words that were powerfully spoken, *"Is there a God? Yes! Is there a Heaven? Yes! Is there a hell? Yes! Are you going to be okay? Yes! Is your Mother in Heaven? Yes!"* The sound of the word "yes" coursed through her entire being! Then these words came to her: *"This is what your mother is feeling right now."* There was no fear; only a sense of pure joy and sincere reverence!

A deep comprehension filled Nancy, imparting to her mind that she was a part of a vast heavenly power! The peace flowed down through her torso, legs, and feet. Almost like an echo, there was confirmation, *"You are a part of it!"* Nancy was amazed, knowing *she was truly feeling what her deceased mother was feeling in the heavenly realm!* As she began to understand the enormity of the experience, Nancy was touched deeply. A sense of humility filled Nancy, along with the reality of God's grace and a new perception of His incomprehensible love for His children. *Nancy Fields was caught up in a rare and magnificent holy encounter with the Almighty living God!*

As if through spiritual telepathy, Nancy comprehended that if she continued her life on earth seeking God through her Christian faith that she too would enter into the holy miraculous peace at the end of her life. Nancy focused her eyes on the small floating white light and she nodded her head as if to say, "I understand." The light moved upward and slightly to the right then faded into the darkness of the night. As the holy feeling gently exited her body through the bottom of her feet, she sat in the chair in complete awe of what happened. It all lasted approximately two minutes, but in a sense it was like an eternity!

Nancy had an intense desire to share everything that just transpired, and at once she went looking for her friend Stacy. Nancy began by saying, "I have something to tell you and I have to say this out loud, now. I don't care if you believe me or not—it does not change the truth about what just happened. I saw a light!"

Stacy looked straight at Nancy and raised her hand. Her thumb and index finger formed a circle and Stacy said, "You just saw a light and it was a brilliant light the size of a silver dollar." Nancy's eyes widened and she was puzzled at first. Stacy continued, saying, "I am your confirmation because I saw it too. It was a light within itself. I was sitting here and this light appeared to me and I felt this wonderful peace and it communicated with me that you were about to have an experience and I was to be your confirmation that this happened. In the years to come, Nancy, you will not doubt what you saw, heard, and felt."

That phenomenal occurrence strengthened Nancy and sustained her through the emotional funeral process during the next few days. In the following months, life without her mom proved to be extremely difficult. Nothing could have prepared Nancy for the tremendous heartache and aloneness she experienced. Settling her mother's estate proved a daunting task and a traumatic undertaking. Nancy needed reassurance as she proceeded through the grieving process. Nancy found herself asking God for a sign that her mother still loved her on two occasions.

God generously complied both times. Once he sent a white pickup truck with tinted windows that drove beside Nancy for a prolonged period in very slow traffic. The word "Ertle" in large black letters on the passenger door loomed before her eyes. Her mom's name was Eartle. That reassured Nancy she was not alone. That is an unusual name and Nancy never saw the name anywhere else before or after that day. (The spelling was slightly different, but the name was the same.) It had to be from God!

A second time Nancy got a sign was when she went to her attorney's office to finalize the estate proceedings. She left there and entered a jewelry store. She looked up asking and promising, "Lord if You will just give me one more sign that Mama knows I handled the proceedings the best way I knew how, I will never ask You for another sign as long as I live!"

Nancy looked down into a ring display and saw a ring bearing the initials EJS. Her mom's name was Eartle Jane Strickland! Nancy bought the ring, placed it on her finger, said "Thank You, Lord," and left the store!

Nancy recalled, "All of this really happened and it was so compelling and persuasive that it still moves me to tears even after sixteen years have passed. I truly know the meaning of humility in comparison to God's awesome power from that experience! God shared a tremendous gift with me that day! I carry that gift with me today and I will carry it with me for the rest of my life. I share my personal testimony with anyone who will listen to me tell of God's grace and promise to His faithful children."

Chapter 3

AN AFTER-DEATH VISIT IN IRAQ

When Lawrence Cheatham died, his absence left a void in his grandson's life. Justin loved his grandfather more than he loved anyone. Lawrence was Justin's hero. He was a big man, standing 6 feet 6 inches tall, weighing 240 pounds. Cancer reduced Lawrence to 168 pounds before he died at the age of 63.

Lawrence had a persona that was bigger than life. "I remember he wore the worst cologne I ever smelled. It was called High Karate, made by Old Spice," Justin said. "When I was a kid, I always told him, 'Grandpa, you smell like High Karate' and he would playfully give me a karate chop across my chest!"

The two of them shared so many good times. When Lawrence died, a part of Justin died too.

"For three years after Grandpa died, I just didn't care anymore. I took unnecessary risks. I did random dumb stuff. I did not do drugs or alcohol but I did stuff like base-jumping. That is where you jump off a tall building or a high cliff side with a parachute strapped to your back. I did extreme kayaking, under extremely dangerous circumstances...I had no fear anymore and perhaps a subconscious desire to be with my grandpa," Justin Cheatham stated.

At the age of 19, Justin joined the U.S. Army. War was raging in the Middle East. Justin said, "I was a 19-year-old, just a scared little boy the first time I was in Iraq. It was a humbling experience, being that young, having someone hand you a gun and a medical bag, saying, 'Here, you are going to war.'"

Before Justin flew out to Iraq, his dad visited him at Fort Bragg, North Carolina. Justin expressed his fears and hesitancy to his dad. Eight people would be counting on him to keep them going if things went bad and he had never shouldered such responsibility. Justin's dad reassured him and expressed his confidence in Justin and his abilities more than once. His encouragement went a long way with Justin, and Justin decided to give the assignment all he had.

When Justin arrived in Iraq, he froze up for some reason. He felt as if he was a kid again and his inner self screamed for some emotional strength and stability.

One night, Justin reached the end of his day feeling extremely tired. He went inside his barracks and he saw his deceased grandfather sitting on the side of his bed. The experience was as real as it could be.

Lawrence wore regular clothing as a deceased being, like the ones he wore in life. He wore a white tee shirt, old wrangler jeans, and red suspenders!

Justin said, "I noticed a fold in the blanket beneath him, caused by the weight of his body. I smelled his cologne, that High Karate I had not smelled in years! We talked, laughed, and joked over the next hour. We hugged and we both shed some tears. He looked as healthy and happy as he did in the prime of his life! The experience did not seem weird or strange and I felt no fear or anxiety. It was all so normal. I felt wonderful in his presence again!"

The deceased Lawrence said to Justin, "Justin, you are going to be all right. You are going to do some great things here and you are going home."

Justin recalled, "Grandpa stood up smiling and started walking toward me. He raised his arm playfully as he did when I was a little boy. He positioned his arm for a karate chop and I expected him to chop me! Suddenly, Grandpa turned and he walked into thin air. He was gone. This is one of those things, when I am ninety years old, I may not remember my own name but I will remember what happened that night!"

Justin spoke to a respected family member back in the states three days later by phone. Justin was amazed when his relative said, "Justin, I want to share something with you. About three nights ago, I had a conversation with your grandfather."

Justin said, "He and my deceased grandfather allegedly talked for several minutes." Justin reasoned about the date and times and discovered the encounters occurred on the same date.

"From that point on, my life changed!" Justin said, "What happened to me was real; strange, but real. I knew I was going to be all right and I knew I was going home! I have never experienced anything like that before or since."

Lawrence's after-death appearance to Justin and his relative helped them understand the magnitude of God's compassion and His love. Those encouraging words Lawrence spoke that night lodged in Justin's heart.

Four days later, Justin was tested. His grandfather's words echoed in his heart, when Justin responded to the crash site of a Chinook helicopter near Fallujah. Sixteen American soldiers died and twenty-six soldiers were injured that day. Military sources later determined that an SA-7 shoulder-fired missile slammed into one of the chopper's rear mounted engines, causing the catastrophe.

Justin recalled rolling on the scene first with his group of GIs. He was the team medic. They got there first to secure the area because it was on the edge of a village. Justin went to work attempting to extricate the casualties from the rubble. He was able to keep some of them alive long enough to make it to the hospital.

The U.S. Army later awarded Justin Cheatham a commendation for his life-saving efforts that day and his accomplishments during his enlistment. The deceased Lawrence Cheatham predicted that Justin would accomplish a commendable act, and in a matter of days that prediction came true.

"Some of the stuff I did there, I don't think I would be able to do again. Some of the things, they are not able to train you for. They cannot train you or prepare you for the devastation you encounter there. I performed like I had been doing that stuff for my whole life," Justin stated.

"I had seven months left in Iraq when my grandpa came back to visit me that night in the autumn of 2003. After that, I went through the rest of my time without fear. I served the rest of my enlistment with courage and confidence. I was always cautious, naturally, but I knew without a doubt that I would be all right. I knew I was going home," Justin stated.

A year after Justin completed his enlisted time in Iraq, he returned to Iraq for a second tour of duty. Later, he deployed to Afghanistan for two tours of duty. The Lord gave Justin peace and assurance of His divine protection under the worst of circumstances. God gave Justin the rare privilege of visiting with a deceased loved one, a privilege he will treasure for the rest of his life.

Chapter 4

THE RUMPF FAMILY:
SUPERNATURAL EXPERIENCES,
1929 TO 1988

PART 1

S arah Alice Rumpf was born in 1863. She lived in Ravine, Pennsylvania, in January 1929 when her life drew near to the end. Family members in the room with her at the time took comfort in what they witnessed in her last minutes. Mrs. Rumpf looked away from the people who were present, looking up, smiling into loving faces that only she could see. Whatever she saw put her at ease.

Mrs. Rumpf began speaking in her native German language, instead of her usual English. She joyfully greeted loved ones as they appeared to her, members of her extended family who had been dead for years! Mrs. Rumpf's family stood by her bedside, watching in amazement as she engaged in conversation with beings visible only to her. Those dearly departed spirits communicating with her obviously came to escort Mrs. Rumpf from this world into the next. Whatever and whomever she saw brought her much joy and filled her with eager anticipation at what lay ahead in the heavenly realm! She died very peacefully.

Part 2

George Elmer Rumpf was the ninth of 15 children born to Johann Jacob and Sarah Alice Rumpf of Ravine, Pennsylvania. He was born in 1899. George's sister, Myrtle (Rumpf) Fisher, was the seventh child in their family. She was born in 1894. Myrtle was in a hospital bed, gravely ill on September 4, 1950, the day her brother, George, died.

Some relatives went to visit Myrtle and saw no harm in telling her that her dear brother had just passed away. Myrtle exclaimed, "How could that possibly be true? He was just here in this room!" George paid Myrtle an *after-death visit* and we will never know what they talked about. Perhaps George described the celestial beauty of Heaven to her! We do know that Myrtle followed George in death just four days after his departure. She died on September 8, 1950.

Part 3

Florence (Rumpf) Culbert, the fourteenth child of Johann Jacob and Sarah Alice, born in 1909, was married and living in a charming little home built by her husband, Edward, and two of her Rumpf brothers. The home was in the mountains of Molleystown, Pennsylvania. Florence was a wonderful, warm, and loving person. She welcomed all of her family members there. In fact, many of Florence and Edward's dear extended family lived in homes on the same lovely mountain road. The extended family thoroughly enjoyed each other's company and frequently visited with each other. Her first grandchild, Peggy Culbert, at the age of five in 1960, held a special place in her grandma's heart. Grandma Florence taught little Peggy to play her first notes on the piano in that cozy mountain home. Music was a big part of Florence's life. Growing up as one of the fifteen Rumpf children, her parents required that each child learn to play the pump organ in their home. They were also encouraged to sing and play band instruments. The possession of a deep love of music and her beautiful singing voice was what Peggy remembered most about her grandmother. Music was such an integral part of her life, along with the joy it brought to her and others dear to her.

Twenty-eight years later, in 1988, Peggy received a phone call from her brother and sister-in-law in Mount Wolf, Pennsylvania. The news was not good. Peggy learned that her Grandma Florence died in a car crash in Florida. Florence and a church friend had gone to visit a relative when a car plowed into their car, killing both of them. That was a devastating time for the whole family because Florence was the matriarch of the family, exhibiting strong faith and character from her Christian upbringing.

Several years prior to her grandmother's death, Peggy began to seriously desire a greater knowledge of God and a clear manifestation of His presence in her life. She felt compelled to pray and ask God for some kind of sign of her grandmother's existence in Heaven. She asked in prayer, and graciously, God sent her the signs she needed!

The first sign happened while Peggy was playing the piano one afternoon after work in the elementary school where she taught music. Suddenly, Peggy saw approximately seven small circles, about four inches in diameter, of pure radiant white light! The light appeared on the wall directly in front of the piano and it flashed repeatedly. It was unlike anything she had ever seen before and Peggy was sure it was from a supernatural origin. The light comforted Peggy and she believed the light was a sign of her grandmother's presence.

The second sign came after the 71st Rumpf Family Reunion on Labor Day Sunday in 1988. All of the family gathered yearly in the rural beauty of the mountainous setting of Hetzel's Lutheran Church picnic grounds in Pine Grove, Pennsylvania. Peggy's grandmother enjoyed the annual gathering particularly because of the wonderful feeling of togetherness that always accompanied the reunions. The family tradition began in

1917 when her parents, Johann and Sarah Rumpf, started it to be certain that all fifteen of their children and their families reunited at least once every year on a happy occasion.

Peggy had prayed for her grandmother to give her a spiritual sign at that reunion. Peggy sat in her grandmother's former living room with her Aunt Christine Culbert, Grandma Florence's daughter, after the reunion concluded. Suddenly a brilliant white light materialized! The light appeared to be two feet wide and over five feet high and it became visible standing beside Aunt Christine! The light appeared as a sheet of solid brilliant white light. The magnificent sheet of light leaned slightly in the direction of Aunt Christine as if it had come to comfort her. The light disappeared after several seconds.

Peggy was so happy for the manifestation and presence of light she saw, and she received it as a visit from the spirit of her deceased grandmother in response to her prayer. Peggy's aunt did not think the exhibition was strange, having felt her deceased mother's presence in the passenger side of her car on several previous occasions when she was feeling extremely sorrowful about her mother's death.

The same Aunt Christine and a friend experienced a holy supernatural incident as small children in St. John's Lutheran Church in Mount Wolf, Pennsylvania. The two children knelt at the altar, praying and seeking answers and comfort from God. They looked up at the cross in the front of the church and both of them saw the form of Jesus hanging on the cross for a brief time. If both had not seen the holy sight, one might have doubted the holy apparition of Jesus they were privileged enough to see.

Quite some time later, Peggy was back in her own home in New Jersey, playing some traditional church music on the church organ in her living room. A bright white light in the form of a woman's silhouette appeared right next to the organ and stood very still, as if listening to the music as Peggy played. The presence caused Peggy to feel like a loving guardian angel was nearby!

Peggy stated, "That was the last significant 'sign' that I remember. I found it very interesting that two of the three visions of white light appeared while I was playing music. They were significant because my grandma's very heart and soul was influenced by music for as long as I can remember. In addition, each experience left me with the intuitive knowledge that all was well. All was as it should be."

Chapter 5

THE ANGEL IN UNIFORM

Dawn Jordan had been looking forward to the well-planned afternoon where she would speak to the parents of football players and cheerleaders before handing out trophies to the children. Dawn was a team mom and she enjoyed participating in the activities of her children. A trip to her physician earlier in the afternoon changed everything for Dawn.

Dawn was 33 years old, a mother of three young children and living near Nashville, Tennessee, when she got the terrible news. She was not emotionally prepared for what the doctor told her. Dawn learned she had breast cancer, and for the rest of the day she tried to act as if nothing was wrong. She felt numb and distraught. Dawn felt tears stinging her eyes but she never gave in to her impulse to cry.

Dawn entered the hospital and a surgeon performed a partial excision of breast tissue that had an excellent chance of eradicating the cancer if caught in time. A short time later, doctors gave Dawn a clean bill of health and a good prognosis.

Seven years later, the cancer returned. Dawn was 40 years old at the time. Doctors advised a surgical breast reduction and chemotherapy. Dawn agreed to take the treatments because she had no alternative. The chemo was called Red Devil chemo and for a good reason.

Dawn experienced side effects of Red Devil chemotherapy—loss of hair, short-term memory loss, severe nausea, loss of appetite, stomach pain, relentless insomnia, and altered mental state with suicidal tendencies. The treatment affected Dawn's body, mind, and spirit. Mentally, she entered a different place, like going into a shell where she could hear what was going on around her although she was unable to interact with those around her.

When Dawn was halfway through the chemo treatments, she reached the point of despair. She found herself in an altered state of mind and she saw herself through the eyes of pain and confusion. Dawn felt like a 14-year-old flat-chested boy because of the loss of her breasts and hair. She could no longer care for her children, and she felt like she was a burden to those caring for her. Dawn's mom, dad, and sister were always there to help her and her three children. Dawn cried continuously, threw up repeatedly, and grimaced from relentless pain. A strong woman up until that point, Dawn could hardly believe that she was contemplating suicide. In her right state of mind, she would never have considered that as an option.

One night when Dawn could no longer tolerate the agony, she got into her van and drove to a remote place where there was a bridge located high above a ravine. She planned to drive her van off the road at that location because she knew she would not survive a crash from that bridge site.

Dawn parked her van and sat sobbing uncontrollably, contemplating her decision. Everything in her knew what she was planning to do was wrong, but she felt unable to fight the thoughts of self-destruction. Dawn wanted the misery to end. She had reached her lowest point in life.

Suddenly Dawn saw headlights behind her car; the car lights suddenly appeared from nowhere, the car did not approach her van. In the next moment, she heard a tapping sound on her window. A man dressed as a police officer stood next to her van and she lowered her window enough to hear his voice.

The man asked, "Can I help you?" He continued talking to Dawn and he seemed to know what she was going through even though she did not tell him. He knew her thoughts and her plan to take her own life. He said, "This is not what you need to do. You need to go home, because you have small children and they are going to need you. You need to finish raising them; they are young and they need their mother. You will be finished with all of this very soon and your life is going to get better. You are going to live; you will be fine." The man then turned and walked away from the car. He did not drive away in the car. He and the car silently disappeared.

"God sent the policeman angel just in time." Dawn confessed, "I did go home that night because I knew God sent an angel to me in the form of a man. God sent the angel to give me hope, to remind me that my children needed me, and to assure me that I was going to live through the ordeal. The Lord even sent the angel in a police uniform so I would feel safe until I realized he was a real angel sent from Heaven! The angel saved my life that night, then the car and the man vanished."

"I lived through the rest of the treatments and I managed to pray for forgiveness. I asked God to allow me to live and raise my children and see my grandchildren, and God gave me everything I asked for," Dawn said. "That is when I came to realize that I was not in control of anything. I understood that God was in control of everything, including me!"

Dawn survived the cancer that almost took her life, but her 30-year marriage did not survive. Dawn stated that her faith in God and God's love for her sustained her during those trials she endured.

She shared her story because she wants others who are going through the same suffering to know without a doubt, "God is watching you and listening to you and He loves you. If you reach the point where you cannot go on, pray. God will help you and He may send you an angel like the one He sent to me. Never give up. God is our refuge and our hope."

Looking back on her life, Dawn remarked, "In the good and bad times, life is all about keeping the faith in God in all circumstances; that is what it is all about."

Chapter 6

MILTON HERSHEY AND HERSHEY GEHRIS

Milton Hershey is known best for his success as the Hershey candy tycoon. Milton Hershey and his wife, Catherine, wanted to be parents. They were unable to have children of their own so they developed an interest in helping orphans. They shared a dream; in 1909, they founded a home and a school for orphaned boys. They called it Milton Hershey School and it was located in Hershey, Pennsylvania.

Mr. Hershey gave all of his personal fortune to the school in 1918. Divine intervention has led approximately fifteen thousand kids to the school over the last 94 years. The truths taught at the Hershey School changed the lives of many of the orphans that ended up there.

Divine intervention is the reason Hershey Gehris, an orphan boy, ended up at Hershey School in the 1940s. He was the oldest of four boys born to parents he described as physically demonstrative and excessive drinkers. As a small boy, Hershey watched his father attempt to take his mother's life on many occasions. He watched his father try to take his own life on three occasions, finally succeeding on the third try.

The year Hershey turned five, his mom decided to place her boys up for adoption, for reasons known only to her. New parents adopted the younger boys right away. No one wanted to adopt five-year-old Hershey. The judge told him, "You're just too old kid; I guess no one wants you."

The child quickly concluded that he needed no one, that he would make it on his own.

Hershey lived in foster care until he was nine years old and he endured many unpleasant circumstances along the way. By his own admission, he was a handful! His rebellion was partly responsible for him leaving foster care, at which time he entered Milton Hershey School for Boys.

The school routinely placed 20 boys in a family setting, in a cottage with two sets of house parents. Boys in sixth grade and above worked on dairy farms. Mr. Hershey believed the boys needed training for the mind, body, and soul. Each boy received training in one of fourteen trades. Young Hershey received training as a carpenter. In addition to an education and a trade, the boys also had extensive training in the Bible, combined with daily devotional times and church on Sunday. Mr. Hershey gave a Bible to each boy and he strongly encouraged the students to read it every day.

Hershey lived at the Hershey school for nine years. He graduated and left that place with the tools to earn a living. He also left with the biblical truths and discipline that came from reading the Bible. Hershey joined the U.S. Marine Corps and served for four years. He married shortly before his discharge and accepted Jesus Christ as his Savior in 1963.

Time passed and Hershey wandered away from faithfully attending church and studying the Bible, and he stopped praying. After fathering two children and being married for thirteen years, he stopped being married and he and his wife divorced.

Hershey remained single for fourteen years. During that time, he felt compelled to begin reading his Bible again the way he did at the Hershey School when he was a child. He decided to read the Bible all the way through once in his life. The Word that he read as a youngster remained in his heart even when he was far from God. That same Word maintained its power, directing Hershey's attention to his sinful nature and the need for change.

Hershey lived his entire life as if he was indestructible. He pushed the limits when he was a Marine, let his marriage fall apart, came close to death in a rodeo accident, crashed while hang gliding, and had a near miss while skydiving when his parachute almost failed to open. The last event, more than anything, reminded him that he was a mortal and that one day he would face death. That event brought him face to face with the knowledge that he would never be safe or truly happy until he surrendered his life completely to Christ.

In 1985, Hershey met a wonderful woman named Dena and married her. Finally, Hershey committed his life to God and returned to worship. He looks back on his early teachers and his benefactor, Milton Hershey, with sincere gratitude.

Hershey said, "I have always believed that I was special to God, not better than anyone, just exceptionally loved by Him. Even when I was far away from Him, I felt His presence. His hand seemed to be forever resting on my shoulder. There was never a doubt that He had a plan for my life. The problem was never with His plan but with my failing to execute it. The Lord loved me when I was unlovable, blessed me when I did not deserve it, and believed in me when I did not believe in myself. He in His wisdom, by Divine intervention, led me to the Hershey School for Orphans, and He used that place and those people to instill His Word in me. Even when I wandered away, that supernatural Word convicted my heart and brought me back to Him."

Chapter 7

SHE WAS CHANGED

John and Elizabeth Shuford considered themselves enormously blessed to have found and married each other. They were very much in love with each other and they understood that love and life are gifts from God. John's dad died when John was only thirteen and his mom died when he was seventeen years old. He learned about the pain of loss and grief at an early age, but John also learned about blessings at an early age. John realized how very much he lost in those two wonderful parents. The loss showed him just how blessed he was to have known them and to have shared a portion of their lives as their much-loved son.

John and Elizabeth learned all about a different kind of love when their two sons were born. Jack and Bradley were born as perfect as they could be. They were beautiful and happy babies! Their mom and dad showered them with love and attention. Each family member complimented the other in ways they could never have imagined until they found themselves living together in a home, as a family!

The Shufords began a new chapter of their lives when doctors diagnosed Elizabeth with colon cancer in 2006 at the age of 39. They experienced shock, disbelief, anger, and acceptance as they searched for the right path to take. Elizabeth entered a difficult world when she embarked on an aggressive course of action, attempting to defeat the cancer invasion of her body. It was not easy on her or John for they waged war on their enemy by committing to a plan of treatment. The treatment came in the form of an attack on the cancer by way of chemotherapy, radiation, surgery, and blood transfusions.

The Shufords traveled to various doctors in various places seeking every reasonable treatment they could find. Treatment began in South Carolina and expanded to Houston, Texas. John worked to earn a living; he became Elizabeth's caregiver, learned new parenting skills in caring for Jack and Bradley and performed cooking and housekeeping. John wore many different hats during those difficult days.

When Elizabeth's condition worsened, John and Elizabeth kept the faith and held the family together one day at a time. The cancer metastasized from Elizabeth's colon to her brain, lungs, liver, and adrenal glands. Some of the treatments Elizabeth endured were almost as wretched as the disease was. She suffered from nausea, vomiting, severe headaches, dizziness, and lethargy. There are no words to describe the physical and emotional toll the wicked disease thrusts upon the patient, the spouse, and the children. Elizabeth endured the treatments because she wanted to live for her boys and for John.

John and Elizabeth's church family and friends bombarded Heaven with a barrage of prayers on their behalf. They helped the family in so many wonderful ways with generous and genuine acts of kindness. John discovered how closely his family drew to the Lord as the situation worsened. He made the assertion that, "Without the pain, most people just don't get it. Those who go through their whole lives with relative ease and no trials and adversity often end up without a clue as to what life is all about. They may even go to church every Sunday but how can they understand what God is trying to teach us? Sometimes, our loss is God's gift to us. The struggles keep us very dependent upon God. He is our strength and provider."

In November of 2007, cancer claimed the life of Elizabeth Shuford. Her greatest concern in leaving this life was the pain her loved ones would feel in her absence. Jack was eleven and Bradley was eight years old when she died. Not all the words in the world can ease the pain of separation in two young boys when their Momma has to leave them behind at such tender ages. Elizabeth was that special woman to her husband and to her two boys. Everyone saw the light in Elizabeth, the caring and doing for others before herself, the sweetness, the unconditional love she exuded, and the emptiness that her departure created in all those who knew her.

The day after Elizabeth passed, John was sifting through her belongings and he noticed an inspirational book that lay on her bedside table. He fanned through the pages of the book and a neatly cut 3 by 3 inch piece of paper fluttered out from between the pages and landed on his shoe. He picked it up to find typed words from the first chapter of the book of James in the Bible. He read, *"Consider it all joy…when you encounter various trials, knowing that the testing of your faith produces endurance. And let endurance have its perfect result, so that you may be perfect and complete, lacking in nothing"* (James 1:2-4).

John wept. He knew God was talking to him. The next day in the mail, John received the weekly newsletter from his church bearing those same precious words from the book of James. It was God's confirmation, reminding him that God was aware of what was happening and He would never leave them. There were many similar confirmations throughout their trial

On March 18, 2008, John went to sleep needing rest, reassurance, and solace. He rarely dreamed, and when he did he was vaguely aware he dreamed and remembered none of the details. That particular night, Jack had his sixth grade play. He played the role of Judas and it was quite a significant role. Jack gave a fantastic performance and John could only imagine how proud Elizabeth would have been if she could have been there. John fought the tears that evening for it was an extremely touchingly occasion.

When sleep did come, John entered a most unusual state of slumber. Sleep was the vehicle that transported John away to the divine location the Heavenly Father had prepared for John and Elizabeth to experience a spiritual meeting of the minds. Upon arrival in that perfect place, Elizabeth descended gracefully from above and she floated toward John. Elizabeth's smile was one of pure joy and her eyes swept slowly across his face. Elizabeth wore radiant white and she was more beautiful than John had ever seen her before. Her skin had the faintest golden glow, while her entire being glowed from the brilliant white light surrounding her!

John said, "The first thing I noticed was that *she was so much more than me.* She had a powerful presence that captured my attention. I was in awe of her. Humility and enlightenment describe what I perceived to a small degree. She possessed a sacred knowledge and confidence because of her enlightenment."

"The second thing I noticed was the absence of verbal communication. We were able to converse with our minds, not our mouths. I 'sensed' all that she was and all she had become as a holy and perfect child of God in Heaven. I knew *she was changed*, having been in His presence."

Elizabeth drifted toward John, never taking her eyes off him, and her smile affected him, holding his gaze. Suddenly, Elizabeth was within his reach and John placed his hands around her lower waist. Elizabeth embraced John and kissed him innocently. Her touch was not a sensual touch but one of deep and sincere love.

With the embrace came a connection by magnetism or electrical energy. A powerful flow of communication flooded John's mind as Elizabeth showered him with her sentiments and her thoughts. Waves of thoughts flowed from Elizabeth, entering John's mind, as she told him, "I am so proud of you, you're doing an amazing job with the children, I am so proud of our kids, and I am so pleased with how things are going." Her thoughts continued, "I love you; I am so happy for you; I am so happy and excited for our children. Most of all, I am so happy where I am. It is wonderful and amazing and I can hardly wait to see you here."

John stated, "Elizabeth appeared to be perfectly content with everything including her present state. She was not interested in returning to earth, as there was no need because she was with us in spirit. There was so much love; there was an outpouring of love emanating from her. It was entirely evident that she was elated with her heavenly existence and her heavenly environment. I understood she was happy about all things—where she was, where the kids and I were, and where we would be in the future. She knew it all. There was no sadness in her, only love, joy, peace, and heavenly, extraordinary contentment."

"In an instant, she broke away, and immediately I sat straight up in bed, wide awake with my heart pounding! It was as if I had heard a door slam! I looked frantically around the room, daring to hope she would be standing beside the bed. My brain naturally began the adaptation process, evaluating the reality or lack thereof of the amazing encounter I just experienced," John exclaimed.

John said Elizabeth's after-death visitation that God so generously allowed affected him in a profound way. "That event is the single most important spiritual moment of my whole life. There is no doubt in my mind about its purpose or its realism. It almost seems like mockery to describe it as a dream. God gifted me by allowing Elizabeth's spirit to visit mine! I can hardly wait to see her again!"

Chapter 8

HEAVEN AND HELL

It appears there is nothing like a little bit of hell to dramatically change life's purpose and attitude.[1]

Most people prefer letting their minds dwell on Heaven more than hell because heavenly thoughts are beautiful and pleasing. Hell thoughts are ugly and unpleasant. The human brain, without prompting, innately knows the difference and sees the reality of the two places. A close review of the Bible makes it clear that Heaven is an extraordinary place and hell is an unbearable place. Let us look at Heaven first.

Then I saw a new heaven and a new earth; for the first heaven and the first earth passed away, and there is no longer any sea.... "Behold, the tabernacle of God is among men, and He will dwell among them, and they shall be His people, and God Himself will be among them, and He will wipe away every tear from their eyes; and there will no longer be any death; there will no longer be any mourning, or crying, or pain; the first things have passed away. ...He who overcomes will inherit these things, and I will be his God and he will be My son" (Revelation 21:1,3-4,7).

Ninety Minutes in Heaven by Don Piper is a true story about a car accident that took his life. Don went to Heaven for an hour and a half before his spirit re-entered his body and he came back to life. In the following sentences, I will share with you some of what he allegedly saw while he was in Heaven.

Don said:

> Age expresses time passing and there is no time there. All of the people I encountered were the same age they had been the last time I had seen them, except that all the ravages of living on earth had vanished. Even though some of their features may not have been considered attractive on earth, in Heaven, every feature was perfect, beautiful, and wonderful to gaze at.

> When I first stood in Heaven, they were still in front of me and came rushing toward me. They embraced me and no matter which direction I looked I saw someone I had loved and who had loved me...I know what the Bible meant by perfect love. It emanated from every person who surrounded me...I felt as if I absorbed their love for me.

> Everything I saw glowed with intense brightness. A holy awe came over me as I stepped forward. I had no idea what lay ahead but I sensed that with each step I took it would grow more wondrous. Then I heard the music...

> Myriads of sounds filled my mind and heart and it is difficult to explain them. The most amazing one was the angel wings...a beautiful holy melody with a cadence that seemed

never to stop. The swishing resounded as if it was a form of never-ending praise.

The praise was unending but the most remarkable thing to me was that hundreds of songs were being sung at the same time, all of them worshiping God.[2]

As for hell and the person who sees no wrong in sin and rebellion toward God, here is what the Bible tells us.

But for the cowardly and unbelieving and abominable and murderers and immoral persons and sorcerers and idolaters and all liars, their part will be in the lake that burns with fire and brimstone, which is the second death (Revelation 21:8).

When considering near-death experiences, I want to point out that we often read far more about positive experiences than we do about negative experiences. I am writing this chapter to draw attention to the fact that both Heaven and hell exist, no matter what we find in print. Based on biblical teachings and near-death experiences, hell is wretched and miserable and it cannot be ignored.

Dr. Charles Garfield, a respected researcher of near-death experiences and author of *Between Life and Death*, noted, "Not everyone dies a blissful, accepting death...Almost as many of the dying patients interviewed reported negative visions (demons and so forth), as reported blissful experiences, while some reported both."[3]

We as human beings find it difficult to admit to failure, therefore, near-death experiences that generate hellish encounters are likely to be neatly tucked away in the recesses of the mind, never to be mentioned by the one who survived the near-death experience.

In 1948, for example, George Godkin of Alberta, Canada related a despairing near-death affair in the midst of a prolonged illness:

I was guided to the place in the spirit world called Hell. This is a place of punishment for all those who reject Jesus Christ. I not only saw Hell, but also felt the torments that all who go there will experience.

The darkness of Hell is so intense that it seems to have a pressure per square inch. It is an extremely black, dismal, desolate, heavy, pressurized type of darkness. It gives the individual a crushing, despondent feeling of loneliness.

The heat is a dry, dehydrating type. Your eyeballs are so dry they feel like red-hot coals in the sockets. Your tongue and lips are parched and cracked with the intense heat. The breath from your nostrils as well as the air you breathe feels like a blast from a furnace. The exterior of your body feels as though it were encased within a white-hot stove. The interior of your body has a sensation of scorching hot air being forced through it.

The agony and loneliness of Hell cannot be expressed clearly enough for proper understanding to the human soul; it has to be experienced.[4]

The description above is horrific but it pales in comparison to the reality and true horrors of hell that are unbearable and unthinkable! The fact that the misery never ends, the separation from God is permanent, the depression and despair from which hell dwellers can never escape forces me to look closely at the matter.

God does not want us to go to hell, but He in His infinite wisdom offers us free will and choices. Why would He want us to be in Heaven if we do not want to be there? Chaos would ensue, much like the earthly scenarios of good versus evil. God does not want anyone to be lost. You and I will choose our own destination. In Second Peter 3:9, we read, *"The Lord is not slow about His promise, as some count slowness, but is patient toward you, not wishing for any to perish but for all to come to repentance."* God does not want us to go into eternal punishment. In spite of His great love for us, however, He is not going to force us to serve Him.

Consider what Dr. Maurice Rawlings wrote in his book, *To Hell and Back*:

> If there is a hell, if the Bible is true...then we must each decide for ourselves, *is it safe to die?* Intriguing the mind and baffling the soul, it is perhaps one of life's most important questions. *The answer lies no more than a few heartbeats away.*[5]

NOTES

1. Maurice Rawlings, M.D., *To Hell and Back* (Nashville, TN: Thomas Nelson Publishers, 1993), 76.

2. Don Piper and Cecil Murphey, *90 Minutes in Heaven* (Grand Rapids, MI, Revell Publishers 2004), 31-32.

3. Robert Kastenbaum, *Is There Life After Death?* (New York: Prentice Hall, 1984), 25, citing G.A. Garfield in Kastenbaum, ed., *Between Life and Death* (New York: Spring Publishers, 1979), 54-55.

4. Marvin Ford, *On the Other Side* (Plainfield: Logos International, 1978), 93-94.

5. Rawlings, *To Hell and Back*, 91.

Chapter 9

TWO MIRACLES
IN ONE LIFETIME

Donna Bard and her husband, Harold, lived in Orrstown, Pennsylvania, when she learned she had Hodgkin's lymphoma, a form of cancer. It was 1969 and treatment for the disease was not as advanced then as it is today. Her physicians recommended that she have chemotherapy and cobalt treatments. The treatment was almost as destructive as the cancer.

Donna refused treatment because she was six weeks away from giving birth to her second child and she did not want to harm the baby. Donna finally gave in to the request of her doctor and a surgeon took the baby a few weeks before the due date. She began cancer treatments days later and she prayed God would allow her to see her children reach the ages of six and nine. Jill and Stephen reached the specified ages and God spared Donna's life; she lived many more years than what she asked for!

Unwavering faith was Donna's greatest asset. She refused to question God when she battled cancer. Throughout the years, various diseases plagued Donna because of the chemotherapy and cobalt treatments she endured in 1969. She battled breast cancer, a damaged heart valve that resulted in open-heart surgery, damaged lungs resulting in severe breathing difficulties, and oxygen usage. Donna faced her trials with courage and she did not complain or question God. Remaining steadfast, she shared her faith and proclaimed her very existence to be a miraculous gift from God.

Donna experienced two distinct miracles in her lifetime apart from God allowing her to live with her physical maladies. She loved to tell the story about the day *God kept her safe in the midst of a storm.*

Donna and Harold had two friends, Ruth and John, who owned a vacation home in Chincoteague, Virginia. Donna and Harold accepted an invitation from their friends to come and visit. Donna decided to go ahead of her husband in hopes she would get some extra fishing time. One day Donna and John ventured out in a small boat to an island in the bay to fish. The weather was fine when they rowed out the morning of the fishing trip.

A sudden storm turned the calm water into a rough sea, bringing boisterous winds and waves to assail the small craft. The boat reeled back and forth and miserably tossed the two occupants about. The threat of death came riding every wave! Donna surveyed the changing sea and prayed for a miracle. It would take a miracle to get them safely back to shore. She prayed, "Lord, show us the way!"

Quite possibly the hand of God Himself touched the water that day from the tip of the reeling boat all the way to shore. *It was as if His finger traced the water in a straight line, forming a pathway, a safe zone for the boaters to follow.* Suddenly, they were able to navigate in calm water between the defiant waves on either side of them! Divine intervention made it possible for them to row safely to the shore. There was no logical explanation for what happened. God saved them. Donna and John made their way to shore and lived to tell that story many times during the course of their lifetimes.

The second episode of Divine intervention in Donna Bard's life happened at a friend's house. Donna's friend, Brenda, welcomed many of her friends to her home monthly to play card games. Everyone gathered in

Brenda's basement where the players exhibited their card game skills while they enjoyed the laughter and conversation. Guests enjoyed the refreshments in addition to the camaraderie.

Donna helped Brenda clear away the snack trays when the party neared the end. She carried the stacked trays carefully, steadying them with both hands. The stairs leading from the basement up to the kitchen did not have a handrail so Donna proceeded cautiously as she ascended. Midway, Donna lost her footing and in an instant realized she was falling backward. The word "Lord" filled her entire being at that moment.

A strong and invisible hand manifested instantaneously, and firmly placed itself against the middle of Donna's back, supporting her as she steadied herself and regained her footing. Donna looked behind her at once but she saw no one. She was alone on the stairs except for the hand of an angel sent by the Lord. A saving hand rescued her at precisely the moment she would have fallen, preventing her from certain injury and possible death. Donna needed no explanation other than surely her Heavenly Father was looking out for her as He had done so often during her entire life!

Against all human odds, Donna lived 41 years from the time she received the diagnosis of Hodgkin's Lymphoma. She watched her children and grandchildren grow up. "A pillar of strength and a tower of faith" is how Donna's family remembers her. God, faith, and family mattered most to Donna. Shining moments where undeniable answers to prayer manifested in Donna's life became part of her testimony. Her strong faith was real and worth sharing. Donna lives on in the hearts of her family and in that place called Heaven.

Chapter 10

BETWEEN LIFE AND DEATH

John Crawford was a land surveyor, living in Orcutt, California when he became the victim of a massive heart attack. John lingered between life and death for nine hours and the ordeal transitioned him into another dimension that he described as "more real than life."

"It was twilight and almost dark when I felt a breeze across my face and opened my eyes," John said. "I was startled to see I was floating above my home and outside my body. I looked down at the gently swaying tops of the pine trees growing along Solomon's Creek behind my house."

At first, John thought he was dreaming, but he quickly realized he was fully awake! The fact that John was floating weightlessly in the sky high above the treetops puzzled him. John looked down and discovered he could actually see through the roof of his home. He focused his eyes on the top of some person's balding head as the man slumped over in an armchair. In an instant, John realized the person in the chair was his own body.

"How is this possible? How did I get up here and out of my body? Am I still alive or am I dead? How do I get down from here?" John questioned literally.

Slowly, John started ascending, not straight up but at an angle. He was frightened and he looked down as he passed over Casmailia Hills. He saw a bright band of silver and gold light shimmering in the darkening twilight far off above the western horizon of the Pacific Ocean.

John's spirit moved upward and he traveled faster and faster until he almost panicked. He had no control over his movements and he did not know how to stop drifting away. His mind began racing and he thought about his wife, Cecile. She was blind and he had not said goodbye to her. At that moment, John cried out franticly, "Please God, someone help me!" He heard the crackling echo of his words disappear through space.

The journey continued and John entered a space of pitch-black darkness. He began moving incredibly fast as if in a vacuum tube or wind tunnel. He felt and heard the roar of wind rushing past him. John grew tired and he entered a sleep state.

After what felt like an hour or even two hours, a flicker of light awakened John. Soon, a small but solid beam of light appeared. The light reeled John in, like a fishing line drawing him closer and closer. The diameter of the light beam grew larger until it reached the same size of the tunnel that transported him.

Suddenly, the wind noise stopped, the darkness vanished, and John entered into the light. It was more brilliant than any light on earth. John sensed he had "popped through" a barrier into an atmosphere made of white light, brighter than earth's daylight!

On the far horizon, John saw a panorama, a sanctuary with a great high wall, glistening like glass. Looking along the face of the wall in both directions, John estimated its length to be endless. The sanctuary was suspended in space and it cast an aura of shimmering golden light, radiating through billowing clouds that rolled continuously.

John willed himself to move forward. He discovered he could move about by controlling his thoughts. John reached the entrance walkway and he saw the source of the beam of light was a standing lion statue, which looked like molten glass infused with gold. The beam of light shut off as if its purpose had been only to guide John to the source of the light.

The pristine figure stood about six feet tall on a low marble pedestal in the middle of a thick, glass-like entrance walkway that was about twenty-five feet wide. The figure did not cast a shadow. John touched the lion and it began wavering, turning translucent and ghostlike. It seemed to be alive and John felt its powerful energy source while standing next to it.

John said, "Underneath the walkway, I saw blue and green colors resembling ocean water, illuminating and flowing lengthwise away from the sanctuary. A simple thought in my mind carried me up the glasslike stairway and across the porch to an open entrance.

"In my lifetime, I had seen some spectacular entrances but that was breathless perfection that one had to see to believe," John exclaimed.

"High above the entrance was a wide stone lintel, supported by a number of white pearl pillars on each side. While standing there, I became mesmerized by the height and infinite length of the sanctuary's massive stone wall, I estimated to be one hundred fifty feet high.

"The wall was golden tan colored and laden with crushed precious stones. They appeared to be emeralds. The sanctuary was constructed like a fortress from an ancient time, of an age I was not familiar with," John continued.

John vividly recalled, "There was an inner sanctuary or refuge, similar to an open Greek portico, and its walk extended through a courtyard to a rotunda built like a domed Greek stoa. In the middle of the rotunda's patio, I was surprised and even intimidated when I came to a deep emerald green headstone that stood about four feet tall. It had a clear jasper, yellowish nose that was rounded and oblong. The facial features were polished smoothly and were almost indiscernible, like a face covered by sheer tightly fitted clinging fabric."

There was some unfamiliar script etched around the face and John was visually inspecting it, trying to read the letters, when he regained consciousness in the hospital. It was nine hours after the heart attack struck him.

John heard the voice of a doctor who was working on him exclaim, "He's back; we've got him back! John, you have had a heart attack. You died when your veins collapsed from a nine unit loss of blood, and we are still trying to save you."

John's swift change of venues confused him, and the sudden realization of his diagnosis and prognosis startled him. He reached out for someone's hand and gurgled, "I'm back, I'm back, please hold tight, and don't let me go again."

John recovered in remarkable fashion in a reasonable period. He began an in-depth study of the Holy Bible. He correlated the scriptures in the book of Revelation, the truth of Heaven as seen and described by St. John's revelation, with what he saw in his near-death experience. John was overwhelmed by the similarities.

He was amazed again when he learned certain things St. John saw were also described by Moses, Ezekiel, and Micah in the Old Testament. Heaven was the place John Crawford believed he had traveled to on his amazing journey. What he read in the Bible simply confirmed it.

It was then that John began to realize the privilege God had given to him. The things he saw were incomparable reminders that strengthened his faith and confirmed to him that the Bible is true. John reaffirmed his belief that our life will continue and Heaven awaits those who sustain their belief in God.

John was humbled and thankful for God's gift of "the visit" and for bringing him back home to his wife, Cecile, and family on earth until it is time to make the second and final journey to Heaven.

John said, "I thank God for boosting and reaffirming my faith by allowing me to visit His kingdom at the 'wall great and high.' His kingdom, built like the fortress at Jerusalem, was floating somewhere out there in the depths of space. I am not exactly sure where it is, but I do know without a doubt, it is there."

John finished speaking by saying, "Everyone must listen. Believe in Jesus Christ. Be attentive to His end-of-days message given to His revered St. John in the last chapter of the Christian Bible. His revelation signals the return of Jesus. It signals the destruction of the evil one, Satan, who did not leave a message or a warning, because he wants to destroy you. This also trumpets the return of 'Messiah' who wants to help you through this lifetime, by way of the cross, to an eternal life in Heaven with God."

Chapter 11

VISITATIONS

PART 1

Gary and Peggy Ferrell of Gallatin, Tennessee, had been married 48 years when Peggy passed away on August 12, 2003. She suffered several strokes over a five-year period from a serious platelet disorder.

Gary was an ordained minister with the General Council of the Assemblies of God and had pastored five churches through the years. He had a very strong faith; however, losing Peggy was the most difficult circumstance he had ever experienced.

The first holiday after Peggy's death was Labor Day, and Gary's children, Lori and Tom, suggested they all get together for a cookout that Monday afternoon. Gary realized holidays were always going to be painful without Peggy because he would face them alone, but he decided he would deal with holidays later.

He chose to spend the afternoon working alone in his yard, trimming shrubs, and cutting the lawn, etc. Gary got his tractor and trailer out to pick up the limbs and debris he cut. His tractor was a John Deer 445 and the engine produced a significant noise. Gary worked from the backyard toward the front as he beautified the yard.

An unusual bird appeared shortly after Gary began working and the noisy tractor failed to frighten the bird away. The bird was very beautiful and it was the size of a pigeon. The bird's feathers were bluish gray and it had unusually large, brown-colored eyes. Gary had never seen a bird like it before.

Everywhere Gary went, the bird followed him, repositioning itself within a few feet of him. The bird watched him with its head tipped a little sideways. Gary at first waved his hand to shoo the bird away, but the bird showed no fear of him. It was persistent, staying close to Gary until he completed his work that day.

When Gary finished his chores and turned off the tractor engine, he knelt down and extended his hand to the lovely creature. The bird hopped over toward his hand, stopping just inches from Gary. Gary spoke softly to the bird, saying, "Come to me little bird; I won't hurt you." The little animal inched closer and closer, turning its head from side to side, steadily gazing up into Gary's face.

Gary spoke, saying, "I'm all right, don't worry about me, everything is going to be okay." Gary thought of Peggy's beautiful brown eyes as the bird studied him with its own brown eyes.

The bird lingered seemingly understanding every word he spoke as Gary continued, "I miss you very much Peggy. I will see you again someday." When he spoke those words, the spell appeared to have been broken. The bird turned and hopped away a short distance. It looked back at Gary one last time, and then flew high into the eastern sky never to be seen again.

Gary felt certain that God sent him an angel that day in the form of a beautiful bird, to encourage him and to remind him that he was not alone!

PART 2

Several months passed and Gary adapted to living his life alone after Peggy died. He was sitting in his home office one day when without warning, Peggy appeared in the hall near the great room. Gary stared in disbelief at first as he focused his eyes on his deceased wife! He was startled!

Peggy looked beautiful! She appeared to be very young, about 18 years old, and in perfect health! She wore a white garment that shimmered with a golden sheen. The robe-like garment did not reach all the way to the floor but it was long. Peggy's hair had no traces of gray; it was a brown color as it had been when she was very young.

Peggy spoke to Gary and she only said his name, "Gary," in the same special way she had spoken it during their many years together.

Gary spoke one word in reply. He exclaimed, "Peggy?" He could not believe his eyes, because Peggy was very much alive, young, healthy, and perfectly beautiful! In a moment, Peggy vanished from sight and Gary sat still and silent. He tried to comprehend that he and Peggy had just made contact in a supernatural way over which he had no control.

Gary called to mind some of the funerals he had preached and he remembered one of his favorite comments. He often asked the question, "Is death where we go to sleep or where we wake up?" The Lord had imparted that powerful statement to him years before. His perspective changed greatly after he saw his deceased wife. The fact that Peggy seemed to want him to know she was all right and doing well gave Gary a great sense of peace!

PART 3

Gary enjoyed being a grandfather and he welcomed visits from his little granddaughter, Carle, who affectionately called him Poppy. Carle loved her Poppy very much and she enjoyed keeping close company with her favorite pacifier at all times! Peggy was the one who went searching for the "passee" when Carle misplaced it. She would shush Gary when he suggested Carle "throw that thing away."

One morning after Peggy died, Gary readied himself for work. He was the chaplain for the Hendersonville, Tennessee Police Department and he was running behind schedule. Carle spent the night with him and he hurried about to get her back to her mom's house before he went to work. Carle's sweet voice rang out in her endearing tone, "Poppy, I need my passeeeee!"

Gary told her to "come on," saying he would just buy her a new one because he could not find the darned thing! He hurried Carle into the small hallway near the door as the housekeeper entered that morning.

Gary was puzzled when he looked at a chair in the hallway where Peggy often sat. He saw a clearly defined impression on the seat of the chair, as if an invisible person was sitting there! The back chair cover had fallen down toward the cushion as it always did when Peggy sat there. The cushion gave way to an invisible source of weight. Gary watched in amazement! The passee rested on the arm of the chair.

Knowing the answer full well, Gary asked his housekeeper, Joann, "Did you put that passee there?" She replied saying she did not, that she had not entered the house, and she did not even know the pacifier was missing.

Gary smiled and shook his head slowly as he recalled a sermon by one of his associates who preached many revivals on the topic called, "Your loved ones are closer than you think."

Chapter 12

CAN YOU SEE JESUS?

My father was only twenty-five years old when he began experiencing unusual debilitating symptoms. He was a very active man. His employment required strenuous physical exertion. He pushed himself to keep working as long as he could because he was the only wage earner in the family.

In November 1953, the day came when Daddy could not get out of bed one morning. He retained so much fluid that he could not even make a fist with his hands nor bend his legs at the knees. His face became very swollen and he had difficulty seeing because the tissue around his eyes became terribly swollen, almost forcing his eyes shut.

Our family lived in a small farming community in Holmes County, Mississippi. As a last resort, Dad was taken to a small hospital for emergency treatment. A general practitioner, Dr. Roy L. Smith, treated him at the hospital and admitted him for testing and treatment.

Each day, Dad grew sicker and more swollen despite efforts by his doctor to make him better. All signs indicated he was dying. Each day, friends visited my father in his room and many of them told him about God and Heaven. He knew he could not continue to live in his condition. He began looking forward to seeing those who visited each day with their Bible stories that gave him hope. He remarked one day, "I didn't come to the hospital to be sick. I came here to have church!"

My mom was at a disadvantage because she had to care for three small children miles away. She did not have access to a phone or a car and she could only go to the hospital when she could get a ride there. It was an incredibly difficult time for the young wife and mother who had to assume all the care and responsibility for her family under those dire circumstances.

Dad's Aunt Louise, the wife of a minister, lived in another town many miles away. Louise offered to come and stay with Dad for several days. While she attended to her nephew, Louise made it her business to share the gospel of Jesus Christ with him and he accepted Jesus.

One night in early December, Dad's condition declined rapidly. His kidneys stopped functioning and he realized he was dying. There was no cure for his disease and dialysis was still unheard of in those days. Kidney failure meant certain death.

Dr. Smith was a compassionate man, he stayed in the room with Dad and Louise as the time of death neared. Penicillin was a relatively new drug at the time and Dr. Smith administered a penicillin injection to his patient not really knowing if it would help at all. Minutes later, Dad's lips began swelling and he complained of difficulty breathing.

He experienced a severe allergic reaction to the penicillin that actually hastened his death and shortened his time of suffering.

Dad told Dr. Smith, "It's feels like I am under a heavy cloud and I can't breathe because the cloud is pressing down against my chest."

Dr. Smith replied compassionately, "Don't worry, I promise you that cloud is about to lift and you will be able to breathe in just a minute."

Louise asked my dad, "Can you see Jesus yet?"

He replied, "Yes I see Jesus, He is right there, can't you see Him? He's right here in front of me." Daddy died moments later, while looking into the face of Jesus by his own admission. Dr. Smith and Louise did not see anyone else in the room but both of them believed the dying man saw the Lord!

My parents had three children and I was the youngest child. I was one year old when he died. I did not know the story about my dad's conversion until I became an adult. I went to work for a general practitioner in Durant, Mississippi, named Dr. Roy L. Smith.

Late in the afternoon, we usually experienced a lull in the flow of patients. When that happened, Dr. Smith frequently came into my office with a cup of coffee. He ordinarily sat in a chair near the front of my desk and each day, he told me a story. He served in the U S Army and was one of the courageous soldiers that stormed the beaches of Normandy in World War II. Sometimes, he shared a war story with me. Other times, he shared accounts of patients he had cared for during his many years of medical practice.

One day Dr. Smith sat quietly, looking out the window, and then he began his story. I enjoyed hearing what he had to say and I respected and admired him very much. Dr. Smith began by saying, "One time, I had a patient and his last name was Moss. Can't remember his first name. He was just a boy." Dr. Smith knew me only by my married name. I said nothing to indicate to him that my maiden name was Moss and he continued.

"The man was as sick as he could be and he stayed in the hospital quite a while before he died. He had chronic pyelonephritis. I gave him a shot of penicillin one night, thinking it might help him. Didn't know he was allergic to it but he was. The penicillin actually killed him but it was a blessing in disguise. He was dying a slow and miserable death, and he just died a little quicker after the penicillin shot. I spent the evening with him, because I knew he was close to death."

Dr. Smith went on to tell me about the cloud my dad saw and how Jesus came for him. He said, "His Aunt led him to Christ."

I said nothing until Dr. Smith finished telling me all the details. At that time I told him his patient was my father. I remember Dr. Smith's face frowned a little and he was silent. After a long pause, he looked at me and said, "You don't say." That was one of his favorite phrases. I nodded my head, yes. I assured him I was glad to know what really happened.

Looking back, God's hand guided me to go to work for that doctor or I would never have known about Dad's conversion experience. I visited my Great Aunt Louise much later in life and she gave me her account of Dad's last days. Dr. Smith has gone on to be with God now. I miss seeing that sweet man who shared so many of his memories with me.

Divine intervention led me to work for Dr. Smith so I could learn about my father's last minutes on earth! God wanted me to know what happened. I have no memory of my dad but I have the knowledge that he was saved. With that knowledge came God's assurance that I will meet him one day in Heaven!

> *I trust in You, O Lord, I say, "You are my God." My times are in Your hands...Your servant, save me in Your unfailing love* (Psalm 31:14-16).

Chapter 13

Unforgettable Ride Down Monteagle Mountain

Monteagle Mountain is not technically a mountain; however, it appears to be a mountain to motorists crossing over it. Monteagle is a section of I-24, between Chattanooga and Nashville, Tennessee. It stretches over the Cumberland Plateau. Monteagle is often referred to as one of the most perilous stretches of interstate in the United States.[1]

Louise Rader[2] was well aware that Monteagle Mountain lay ahead of her. She did not mind going up the mountain; it was the steep downhill grade that troubled her. She was an excellent driver but had never driven that stretch of road in an unfamiliar, manual transmission rental truck loaded to capacity. Louise's mom and dad moved to Florida when they retired, searching for a warmer climate. Her dad died suddenly only months after the move, leaving her mom alone in a strange environment. Louise offered to move her mom's home furnishings back to Nashville if her mom could hire movers to load the truck.

The estimated twelve-hour trip turned out to be an exhausting journey. Louise discovered she was not as confident behind the wheel of the fully loaded big truck as she thought she would be. The going got tough but Louise had no choice except to keep going.

Daylight was fading fast when Louise reached the beginning of the incline on Monteagle Mountain. She was apprehensive and drove very cautiously. She had heard stories about professional big rig drivers who encountered trouble on that treacherous road and that knowledge was unsettling. Traffic was light and that was in her favor.

The downhill slope seemed to get steeper by the second and the weight of the load she was carrying did not help matters. Louise attempted to slow the truck down but her efforts were futile. She picked up speed in spite of all her efforts slow down. The brakes alone simply could not stop the truck and Louis knew she was in for a horrific crash! She smelled burning rubber and she wondered when the brakes would fail completely. Her white-knuckled hands locked on the steering wheel.

Louise could only think, "Daddy would know what to do!" Sheer panic seized her and she screamed aloud, "Daddy *help me!*"

At that moment, Louise heard her dad's voice. She turned toward the sound of his voice and was startled to see her deceased dad sitting in the seat next to her. His calm voice reassured her, telling her, "You can do this, Louise, I know you can do this. Stay calm and do exactly as I tell you to do."

Louise listened and obeyed each command he spoke, clutching and downshifting in accordance with her dad's instructions. Finally, the out-of-control truck slowed down to where Louise was sure she was in control of it again. She released her clenched jaws. She could breathe again. Her heart was racing and Louise knew God just sent her dad and He saved her life. Taking her eyes off the road for just a split second, Louise glanced over to say thank you to her father. The seat was empty. Her dad had disappeared as quickly as he had appeared.

Louise drove the remainder of the descent in a lower gear and maintained control of the vehicle. For the rest of the trip, Louise thought about her dad! He was dead but he was alive, and he was in the cab of that truck with her for a brief time. She came close to dying that evening and she knew God sent her dad to talk her through the steps she needed to take to slow the truck down. When Louise saw her dad's face and heard his voice, she regained her confidence and composure. She could hardly comprehend it all. Louise could not stop smiling! She prayed, offering many thanks to her Heavenly Father that night. She reminded herself, in life or in death, "I will always be Daddy's girl!"

Notes

1. "Monteagle Mountain," from *Wikipedia The Free Encyclopedia.*

2. This is a true story, but the names were changed to comply with a privacy request.

Chapter 14

CEMETERY VISIT IN HAMBURG, IOWA

Gail Clover was only 14 years old when she experienced the loss of one she truly loved. Mabel Haith had raised Gail's mom, Barbara, in the absence of her real mother. Gail thought of Mabel as her grandma. Mabel died of a heart attack. She was a very special woman with endearing qualities. Mabel was loving, generous, and kind. Her passing was a great loss to those who loved her so much.

On Memorial Day in 1963, Gail accompanied her mom and her grandfather to visit Mabel's grave. They drove to Mabel's home in Auburn, Nebraska to gather flowers from Mabel's garden to take to the cemetery in Hamburg, Iowa. Gail walked through the garden, picking flowers and remembering how much she loved and missed Mabel.

Gail prayed, saying, "Dear God, please let Grandma know we are bringing her flowers today." Gail and Barbara picked a very large bouquet of red, white, and pink peonies and placed them in the trunk of the car before they drove away that day.

Beautiful blue sky and an occasional strip of white stratus clouds high in the sky captured Gail's attention. The distant beauty caused her to think of Heaven and Grandma Mabel. The family arrived at the cemetery in Hamburg. Gail and Barbara were talking and taking in the beauty of the surroundings when Barbara abruptly paused. Looking toward Mabel's gravesite, she exclaimed, "Gail, who does that look like to you?"

Gail looked directly at the spot where Mabel's body was buried; seeing Mabel standing near her own grave startled Gail. Mabel's eyes were downcast and she appeared to be admiring the existing flowers on her own grave. Gail sat still; she was awestruck!

Floyd, Gail's grandfather, watched in disbelief and started to cry as he stared at Mabel in amazement. Barbara, Floyd, and Gail watched in silence at first. The deceased Mabel turned and looked at her family with a peaceful expression. Gail could not take her eyes off her Grandma as she attempted to comprehend how she could be looking at a woman whose funeral she recently attended.

Gail noted that Mabel was wearing a black and brown striped house-dress, identical to one she had worn in life. There were large buttons down the front of it. She carried her purse tucked under her arm, which was characteristic of her. In life, Mabel always stood erect with shoulders back in a regal manner and she stood that way by the grave. Her hair was the same beautiful auburn color.

Barbara and Floyd got out of the car and began taking flowers out of the trunk. Barbara asked Gail to get out of the car and Gail refused. She could not understand how her grandma could be both dead and alive. Barbara responded to Gail's refusal by saying, "She wouldn't hurt you when she was alive, and she is not going to hurt you now." Barbara may not have understood what was going on by the after-death appearance, but she did not doubt that Mabel was somehow very much alive at that moment.

Reluctantly, Gail exited the car and they gathered all the flowers and closed the trunk of the car. All three of them began walking toward the grave and as they walked, Mabel vanished. She was gone.

Three witnesses saw Mabel Haith standing beside her own grave. Three people agreed that it was no apparition, that Mabel was real and alive. Her facial features were clearly defined and vivid. All three observers described the clothing Mabel wore and all three observations were identical. Each of them saw her beautiful auburn hair. Barbara, Gail, and Floyd left the cemetery shaken and stunned because of what they experienced. Not one of them could explain it but they would never doubt they saw it. They never forgot what they saw.

Many years have passed since that miraculous day and Gail looks back on that encounter with great appreciation and enthusiasm! She remembers her simple prayer in the flower garden. Gail asked God to let Mabel know they were taking flowers to her grave. In answer to that prayer, Gail believes the Lord sent Mabel to see the flowers, as confirmation that He heard and answered her prayer! Gail has often wished she could see her grandma again; however, that day was the first and last after-death appearance by Mabel Haith. Gail is ever mindful of the reunion in Heaven that awaits all who believe!

Chapter 15

MINNESOTA TRAGEDIES

Krista Lindquist recalled the devastation of the summer of 2006. Krista's boyfriend, Jake, was in a serious diving accident. Jake's neck was broken and the accident left him paralyzed from the chest down. The injuries changed both their lives in many ways. Jake ended up at a medical facility in another state. Krista adapted to the tragedy in her own way and with great difficulty.

Several months later, Krista entered a relationship with a friend from her childhood. His name was Cody, and when Krista was with Cody her pain and depression seemed bearable. They fell in love, but their happiness was short-lived.

Krista and Cody were involved in a horrific car accident one night. The impact of the single car collision hurled both of them from the rear seat of the car through the back window and onto the ground. Cody's body broke the glass and exited the window first; he sustained massive injuries. Krista's body exited through the car window after him although she had been wearing a seat belt. Two other passengers in the front seats of the car sustained mild injuries.

Separate helicopters airlifted Krista and Cody to St. Mary's Hospital in Duluth, Minnesota that night. Cody died before he reached the hospital. Krista arrived at St. Mary's alive with severe bruises to her body and serious injuries to her liver and spleen. Her lower lumbar spine received several small fractures. Krista was cared for in the Intensive Care Unit initially, then in a regular hospital room where she made a full recovery over the next few weeks.

Krista's body healed well; however, her heart remained broken. Her emotional well-being suffered because of her painful experiences in the previous months. She had once loved Jake and she lost him. Krista loved Cody and she lost him as well. She was not emotionally equipped to deal with the incidents that changed her life.

Cody's death left Krista with an odd curiosity to know what happens at the time of one's death. She could not deal with losing Cody, and she wanted to discover where he really was since he died. Krista decided she would take her own life at the site of the accident on the first anniversary of the crash. She tried to ease her pain with drugs for a while but that only made matters worse.

A series of unfortunate events led Krista to an emotional summer night filled with anger, depression, and regrets. Krista got into her car and drove toward the site of the accident where she intended to kill herself. She felt a sick sense of excitement as she headed out on the highway on a disturbing journey, fueled by her decision to end the pain the only way she knew how.

Approximately one mile away from Krista's destination, she experienced an overwhelming sense of someone's presence in the car with her. Krista suddenly became aware that someone was sitting in the passenger seat beside her. From the lights on the dashboard, she could see Cody sitting beside her with his hands in his lap the way she had seen him sit beside her when he was alive. Krista could see Cody more clearly in her peripheral vision. She noticed his appearance diminished to a glowing mist each time she looked directly at him. Chills ran over her body as she realized Cody was alive again and sitting next to her in the car.

Cody spoke forcefully to Krista saying, "Krista, go home! Krista, go home!" Krista was shaken and she pulled the car to the shoulder of the road and got outside where she stood trembling and sobbing. Above the sound of the wind and the passing cars, Krista heard Cody's voice once again commanding her, "Krista, go home! Go home!"

Krista caught her breath and she looked up at the stars in a purple night sky. She then experienced an overwhelming sense of calm and peace that was unlike anything she had ever felt before. Composure returned to Krista and she managed to pull herself together and digest what just happened. Cody, who was deceased, had returned to keep her safe. The anger and hurt over circumstances beyond her control dissipated and Krista drove home as Cody told her to do. The after-death appearance by Cody prevented Krista from ending her own life.

More than five years passed since that night when Cody saved Krista's life. Krista settled into her life with a beautiful baby girl named Jaelyn. After some soul searching, Krista finally reached a place where she surrendered her life to God, and by her own account she said, "I have found the last piece to my puzzle, in finding a real relationship with God and an understanding of His gifts of life and death."

Chapter 16

JAN, DIANE, AND KELLY: SMOKEY MOUNTAIN MEMORIES

Each year, Jan Richards and her two sisters, Kelly and Diane, traveled from middle Tennessee to the Great Smokey Mountains for a time of fun and strengthening of family ties. At 32 years old, Diane had a strong faith and a strong sense of humor. Diane tried to make light of the fact that the pain in her back had become a way of life; she was not a complainer.

The sisters arrived in Gatlinburg and as soon as they unpacked, Diane insisted the three of them should go to the nearby photo gallery! Diane chose a vintage outfit consisting of a long flowing dress; it was a floral print and mauve colored. She selected elbow-length black lace gloves and a mauve-tinged hat ornately decorated with a feather. She posed for the camera and the flash left her seeing spots before her eyes. Minutes later, Diane carefully inspected the black and white photograph and she laughed at her own likeness. She appeared to be from another era, 150 years before.

Before the vacation ended, Diane's sisters became very concerned about the persistent pain and they insisted she see a doctor as soon as she got home. Diane did seek medical attention and diagnostic studies revealed that Diane was in the final stage of T-cell lymphoma, a deadly disease. Diane endured chemotherapy and ultimately ended up at St. Thomas Hospital in Nashville for her final days.

On one occasion, Diane reported seeing an angel in the corner of her hospital room although no one else could see it. Diane's family rarely left her alone; however, one day she was alone for a brief period. During that time, an unusual group of men visited her. A nurse sat at a station near Diane's door, but she saw no one enter Diane's room. Diane said four men suddenly appeared around her bed. They were elderly men and they wore outdated suits. Diane asked which church they were from; one of them replied they were "traveling" men. The men got on their knees and each man prayed for Diane. When the prayer ended, Diane opened her eyes as soon as she heard the word "Amen." The men were nowhere in sight. Diane accepted the fact that they really were "traveling" angels and she received comfort by the appearance. Diane died a few days later with her husband Bill at her bedside.

Diane's husband, Bill, went into Vanderbilt Hospital only a short time after she died. Bill had a surgical procedure on his brain that his doctor performed to treat his epilepsy. Diane's nephew, Randy, was at Bill's bedside when the hospital room door burst open! A lively-stepping woman wearing vintage clothing and a hat with a feather pranced up to Bill's bedside and made a bold announcement. The woman said, "He is going to be all right. He is going to be okay!" The woman was Diane! She exited the room as quickly as she appeared. Diane had announced those same exact words to Bill when he went in the hospital for treatment way back before she became ill.

Randy's mouth fell open but he was shocked into silence! Randy leapt out of his chair and hurried after the woman. He entered the hall right behind her but the woman was nowhere in sight. Nurses just outside the door to the room never saw her enter the room. Randy called Diane's sister, Jan, and explained what happened.

Jan's mind raced and she thought of the Gatlinburg photograph! The photo was in black and white and no one except the sisters knew the colors of the ensemble. Jan asked Randy to describe the outfit and the colors he saw. When Randy described the mauve-colored ensemble down to the last detail, Jan shivered. She knew her deceased sister had just visited and delivered a message of hope to her husband Bill. Jan did not know how this could happen; however, Bill and Randy both witnessed the event and the accurate description of colors confirmed the after-death appearance. All who learned about the visit were encouraged. Bill recovered, left the hospital a few days later, and he was seizure free. The surgery was successful, just as Diane predicted!

Chapter 17

HARRY AND ANNE IN BROOKLYN, NEW YORK

PART 1

Harry and Anne Gabber were married in 1938. They lived in a modest apartment in Brooklyn, New York. Franklin D. Roosevelt was president of the United States in 1938 and the average home price was 545 dollars. The minimum hourly wage was 40 cents per hour for a 44-hour workweek. The average cost of an automobile was 763 dollars. A loaf of bread cost 9 cents and a gallon of gasoline cost 10 cents in those days.[1] This gives you an idea about the world in which Harry and Anne lived. Anne gave birth to three beautiful daughters—Rosemary, Joan, and Stephanie. Harry worked the night shift in a paper-boxing factory to support his lovely family.

Harry went to bed one night in a very ordinary way; however, he did not wake up the next morning. At the age of 54, Harry suffered a massive heart attack while sleeping and he died. Harry's death devastated Anne and she found herself in a difficult place. She had never worked outside the home and circumstances forced Anne to find work to support herself and her family. Working and caring for her family was very necessary but it was a task not easily accomplished.

A short time after Harry died, Anne awoke from sleep one night and discovered she was not alone. Anne could hardly believe what she saw! She saw her deceased husband, Harry, standing silently at the foot of the bed. He looked very healthy. He did not speak; he was silent as he looked into Anne's eyes. Anne called out to Harry but he did not reply. He simply faded out of sight. Seeing him gave Anne a great deal of hope. She had discovered that life on earth was not always easy, but seeing Harry made her smile. Just thinking about Heaven without all the earthly trials gave her much to look forward to.

Anne treasured the after-death appearance in her heart and she pondered what she saw. She comprehended that Harry was still very much alive although he was obviously in a different, holy realm.

PART 2

In 1962, Anne's health declined and her physician recommended that she have a complete hysterectomy. Anne agreed to the operation but she tolerated the surgery poorly. She lost a lot of blood. Anne became very weak and infection spread through her body. She ran a very high temperature for many days because of the infection. Anne nearly lost her life during that illness, and one night while she was at her weakest point, she obviously died and her spirit temporarily left her body. Anne later told others about her near-death experience and she described it as a dream-like experience. What she described was typical of a near-death experience.

When Anne's spirit left her body, a powerful force propelled her into a corridor, through a very long and dark tunnel. She could see there was a very bright light at the end of the tunnel. Anne reached the end of the tunnel and when she emerged, she was delighted to discover a number of men and women all around her who appeared to be in the same state of being as she was. All the people walked toward a beautiful body of water!

A man stood next to a boat at the edge of the water. Anne questioned the man as to whether or not she should get in the boat. The man told Anne she should not get in the boat; he said it was not her time. The man gently told Anne that she should go back to where she came from.

Anne's fever mysteriously broke early the next morning, the infection left her body, and she recovered from the surgery and complications. A trip to the edge of Heaven seemed to have a healing effect on Anne's earthly body. She made a full recovery!

PART 3

Anne lived a long and full life. When she was more than 80 years old, her heart became very weak. Anne required full-time rest and nursing home care when her condition deteriorated. Anne's oldest daughter, Rosemary, was with her when she approached her last hours on earth. Anne spent many hours tossing and turning restlessly. She was in apparent distress.

Suddenly, Anne unexpectedly sat straight up in bed! She looked past her daughter, focusing on someone just behind her with great anticipation. Anne appeared to have seen a familiar and beloved face! Rosemary turned to see who was there behind her but she saw no one. Anne faced death at any moment; however, her face lit up and a smile changed her entire countenance! Her expression was one of pure happiness and peaceful bliss. Rosemary could only assume her mom saw a smiling face and extended arms that reached out for her to lead her home.

Anne lay back at that very moment and closed her eyes as her spirit left her body. She died peacefully.

Anne and Harry were never rich by earthly standards, but their daughters always felt richly blessed by having shared their lives with two of the most worthy people in the whole world!

NOTE

1. www.thepeoplehistory.com/1938

Chapter 18

GOD'S SECRET AGENT ANGELS IN LEBANON, TENNESSEE

Aaron White took his time crawling out of his nice warm bed that cold, rainy morning. By all appearances, February 29 was shaping up to be a typical wintery day in Lebanon, Tennessee. Aaron chose warm, layered clothing that morning. He got dressed, then went into the kitchen to eat breakfast.

Aaron's grandmother, Jan, was already in the kitchen having her third cup of coffee when Aaron sat down at the table. Jan's devotional lay open on the table and the reading for February 29 was very prophetic. Before the day was over, the devotional reading would echo in Jan and Aaron's hearts in a powerful way!

The exact wording of the devotional reading was, "God has His own secret agents—angels. God's angels never fail in their appointed tasks. We will never know how many accidents were avoided because God's angels protected us."

For He will give His angels charge of you to guard you in all your ways (Psalm 91:11 RSV).

Aaron and his sister had an uneventful ride to school that morning. When Aaron prepared to leave school in the afternoon, he learned his sister had made plans with a friend and would not be riding home with him as usual.

Aaron drove to the home of a relative where his dad, Randy, was making a repair on a car. They talked a few minutes before Aaron decided to drive home. He was only 17 at the time and the road condition was wet and slippery. Randy chose to follow Aaron to make sure he arrived home safely.

The road home consisted of several turns and traffic lights and one very significant curve. One traffic light detained Aaron's dad, creating a slight distance between the father and son. Aaron drove a white 1997 Camaro that day as he approached the curve. Aaron's car fishtailed on the wet pavement, causing him to lose control of the vehicle.

Aaron heard a horrific crash of metal crushing metal and glass breaking. When Aaron lost control, his car swerved to the left, placing him in the immediate path of an oncoming black Camaro traveling at 50 miles per hour. The oncoming car struck Aaron's car in the center of the passenger side.

Sheer terror overwhelmed Aaron as he looked around in shock, trying to figure out what just happened. He looked down and noticed his feet were bare. The impact knocked his socks and shoes off his feet! All the glass in the car was broken out except for one window. Aaron unbuckled his safety belt and he managed to crawl through a window to free himself from the demolished car.

When Aaron stood up, he realized something was very wrong. He was extremely weak and shaking but he did not realize the extent of his injuries. He sustained fractures of the shoulder, the pelvic bone, and jawbones. The left side of his face suffered severe lacerations and the broken bones of his jaw protruded through the gaping facial wounds. Aaron clung to the side of his vehicle attempting not to fall down. Waves of nausea flooded his body.

Suddenly, an older man appeared next to Aaron. The man looked to be around 60 years old. His hairline receded and his hair was gray.

He needed a shave. The Good Samaritan stood quietly and very close to Aaron. He placed the palm of his hand against the center of Aaron's back. Some unexplainable force joined his hand and Aaron's back. The force of energy from his hand strengthened Aaron and steadied him, giving him the ability to remain standing with strength that had not been present only moments before.

Aaron frantically looked around and for the first time, he caught sight of the car that hit him and he saw the female driver of that car lying on the pavement. The woman's car caught on fire. A wave of panic surged through Aaron and the silent man spoke for the first time, saying, "You're going to be okay, son; you're going to be okay." The quiet stranger rubbed Aaron's back and the kind gesture soothed and comforted Aaron. A strange peace filled Aaron's mind and the panic subsided.

Randy arrived moments later and he ran to his son. He later stated that he saw no man near Aaron. Aaron turned to find his helper had vanished. He was gone. Aaron's dad could not imagine whom Aaron was talking about when he tried to explain about an angelic man who calmed him and helped him through those first terrifying minutes.

Aaron landed in the trauma center at Vanderbilt Medical Center in Nashville where surgeons worked for eight hours to reconstruct his face. Prompt medical attention and time healed Aaron's other broken bones over a period of several weeks. The driver of the other car lived and recovered from her injuries. Aaron's sister survived that day because God protected her and He redirected her path the afternoon of the accident.

Aaron never doubted that God spared his life and an angel cared for him because ordinary people cannot just disappear! The old man who needed a shave did not have wings nor did he wear white garments. Angels come in various forms but they are still angels. God really does have his own secret agents!

Chapter 19

FINDING LOVE,
AFTER ALL THOSE YEARS

Maxine Fields-Mitchell, full-blooded Cherokee Indian, was a small woman in stature, standing at only four feet and eleven inches tall. After a brief conversation, it became apparent that the 80-year-old was a woman of extraordinary faith and superior intelligence. Her mind was as sharp as an 18-year-old. She enjoyed telling the story of how the Lord miraculously intervened in her life, orchestrating circumstances that led her to marry Josie Mitchell in her later years.

Josie Mitchell was a Muscogee Creek-Seminole Indian. He began preaching full time after he survived the terrorist bombing attack at the Oklahoma City Federal Building in 1995. He went about preaching and sharing his testimony. He told about the miraculous encounter he had with an angel who saved his life the day of the attack. His wife died in that same attack and Josie led a lonely life after that incident.

Josie was asked to preach the funeral of a young man approximately a year after the bombing. At that funeral, Joe encountered a man named Tony Fields. Josie shook Tony's hand and stared into his face for several seconds.

Josie said to Tony, "You look so familiar, do I know you? Remind me who your parents are?"

REAL MESSAGES FROM HEAVEN

Tony told him his parents were Sam and Maxine Fields. Josie laughed loudly and exclaimed, "I knew it, I knew it! I saw the resemblance. I always knew that Sam Fields would go after my girl after I left Bacone!"

Sam was a full-blooded Muscogee Creek Indian. He and Maxine both attended Bacone Indian School in Muskogee, Oklahoma in the early 1950s. Bacone Indian School was a boarding school. Adjacent to the boarding school was Murrow Indian Orphanage and the children from the orphanage attended Bacone. Josie and Sam had both lived at the orphanage while Maxine stayed at the Baptist Indian Boarding School. Josie and Maxine had been boyfriend and girlfriend up until the time Josie left there to attend Haskell Indian Boarding School in Lawrence, Kansas because of his athletic abilities as a boxer.

When Josie left, Sam and Maxine began dating and remained close until they graduated. The two eventually married and had three children together. Many years later, Sam and Maxine's marriage ended in divorce and Maxine moved to and worked in Arizona at the Department of Indian Services. Maxine had recently moved back to Oklahoma City in 1995, just prior to the "chance" meeting between Josie and Tony Fields. Maxine had diligently sought the Lord's direction in her life, realizing she was alone and without a clear direction of what she should do with the remainder of her years.

Divine intervention was the reason for that meeting, after all those years, according to Maxine. The meeting between Josie and Tony led to Josie and Maxine's reunion and them getting married after a 50-year separation. When the couple said their wedding vows, Josie said, "It took me 50 years to get her back, but I knew one day I would get my girlfriend back!"

After the wedding, Josie and Maxine settled in Oklahoma City and they were very happy together. Josie became a pastor of a small church in Enid, Oklahoma and the couple traveled over a hundred miles each week to deliver his sermons to the congregation. Regrettably, Josie died suddenly in May of 2007. Maxine, clearly the matriarch of her family, remains active today, telling others about salvation through Jesus Christ and how God intervened in her life in answer to her prayers, because of her faith.

Chapter 20

His Spirit Looked Like His Body

Carole Smith[1] returned to middle Tennessee in early winter because her father was gravely ill with lung cancer. Her dad, Carl, had struggled to breathe and he courageously endured the increasing pain because his wife and three daughters wanted him to live so badly. The truth was, he was tired of fighting and he wanted to go home to Heaven.

Carole's dad had decided to request pain medication to make him comfortable so that he could die in peace. His doctors had informed him there was nothing else they could do to help him. They agreed with the decision he made to ease the pain.

After spending one afternoon and one night with her dad, Carole understood his decision and she wondered how he had endured as long as he had. She loved him very much and she did not want him to suffer beyond what he could stand. When nurses began administering the strong painkiller, Carl slipped into a quiet sleep and he did not awaken during the next two days.

It was late afternoon when Carl's family noticed his breathing pattern had changed. His heart rate slowed and changed significantly. They knew his death was imminent. Carl's wife and their three daughters sat near the bed. All the words had already been spoken. There were silent tears and heartbreak as they watched the life slip away from the one they loved so much.

Suddenly, Carl sat straight up in the bed. At least that is what his family initially thought. He swung his legs over the side of the bed and sat looking at his wife. He smiled without saying a word. He turned to Carol and smiled at her, and then he turned to each daughter and smiled. He spoke no words.

Carl placed his feet on the floor and stood up. His stunned family watched in disbelief, because at that moment they could clearly see that Carl was also lying flat in the bed and he appeared to be dead.

Carl's spirit stood up and walked between them, walking directly toward the wall near the foot of the bed. When he reached the wall, he did not slow down. He walked through the wall and the family saw him no longer. His human body remained in the bed and they quickly comprehended that his spirit just left his body and smiled at each of them before he left the room. His spirit looked exactly like his body!

Carl's family could not speak for several seconds because they could not believe what they just saw; however, all four of them saw the same thing! The supernatural vision they just saw made them feel overjoyed while they were still feeling the pain of losing him.

Later on, each family member felt incredibly blessed by the experience. They were not sure others would believe them. What they saw was real and the memory comforted them in an amazing way through the months that followed. The women no longer have any fear of death. They are Christians as Carl was, and they look forward to going to Heaven when it is time with no apprehension.

NOTE

1. This is a true story, but the names were changed to comply with a privacy request.

Chapter 21

TWO DECEASED RELATIVES
CAME TO VISIT

Treva Ferrell and her husband, Eldie, lived in McMinnville, Tennessee. They owned and operated two businesses that required much time and work. Treva was a busy woman and she tried to dismiss the fact that she was sick until she awoke one morning and could barely breathe. Treva sought medical attention and her doctor saw that she was in trouble. He promptly admitted her to the hospital for treatment.

A short time after admission to the hospital, the doctor diagnosed Treva with congestive heart failure, pulmonary edema, aggressive atria fibrillation, and pneumonia. Treva's prognosis was grim. Her doctor said she would not live for more than two days.

Doctors aggressively treated Treva with powerful medication and she lived in spite of predictions. The third night of Treva's hospitalization, she experienced something very unusual. Treva lay on her side, facing the wall of her hospital room. By her own admission, she felt like she was dying. She only wanted to be left alone so she could rest. She was quietly resting there in the hospital bed when she heard a voice coming from behind her.

A man's voice whispered her name and she ignored it. She was too weak to talk to anyone. The voice called a second time and she still ignored it. The voice called her name a third time and Treva knew someone was standing just inches from her back. She reluctantly turned over to see who it was and what she saw shocked her! She found herself face to face with her dad and her aunt! Treva was shocked because her dad and Aunt Lee had been dead for years!

Treva's dad appeared strong and large in stature, as he was in his younger days. She saw him as clearly as when he was alive. He wore his hair thick and combed straight back the same way he always did. He wore a black bowling shirt with pleats on the side and his name above the pocket. Treva noticed each detail.

Aunt Lee's face was a bit hazy but her voice was the same. She wore a pink three-piece linen suit. Treva's dad spoke clearly and he said, "Treva, come on," indicating she was to go with him. Treva refused and her dad repeated his request. Each time, Treva refused and asked her dad to leave her alone. Her dad then spoke firmly to her and in a very demanding tone he said, "Come on, Butch!" Treva yelled in response and refused to go with him. Aunt Lee laughed in her jovial way before they both disappeared. Treva wondered why he called her Butch.

Treva called for a nurse and asked if any of her medication could cause her to hallucinate. The nurse assured her that was not the case and wanted to know who she was talking to earlier. Treva was upset but she no longer felt resigned to accept her death fate. Her fighting spirit emerged and she grew stronger from that point on. She was not going anywhere against her will! The nurse returned with two pills to help her calm down enough to sleep.

When Treva woke up the next morning, her husband, Eldie, was by her bedside. He said he had to know how she was. He went home the night before to get some rest. A conversation began and revealed that while Treva's after-death appearances were in progress, two angels were visiting Eldie.

Two angels appeared in the room just moments after Eldie got into his bed. He saw two separate angels who were hazy in appearance but dressed in white. They spoke but Eldie did not understand the words they spoke. The angels disappeared as abruptly as they appeared and Eldie knew he should call the hospital. He thought they had come for Treva. Nurses told Eldie that Treva's condition had not changed; she was no better and no worse.

Treva experienced a sudden change for the better following the after-death appearances. She left the hospital and recuperated at home, making a full recovery. Treva's mom, Lucille McCluskey, came to her home to help care for her and they engaged in a very interesting conversation.

Treva learned her brother had a photo of her dad in the same black bowling shirt he wore the night of his visit. Lucille reluctantly admitted that her husband called Treva Butch when she was a tiny girl. Lucille convinced her husband to refer to their daughter by her given name and he stopped calling her Butch when she was very young. The conversation served as confirmation to Treva that her visit with her dad and aunt was real. Eldie's encounter with two angels also served as confirmation that something supernatural had taken place. Treva remained in a state of awe for some time because she never realized such things were possible!

Treva had to admit, she reclaimed her fighting spirit to survive when her dad insisted that she leave this life with him. Before he came, resignation settled on Treva and she only wanted relief. She was ready to give up. Treva gained contentment from the knowledge that her dad knew exactly what to do and say to encourage her to fight the sickness that almost took her life!

Chapter 22

GRANDPARENTS' GOODBYE TO APRIL SHARP

PART 1

April Sharp of Lebanon, Tennessee, recalled with sadness the early morning that her grandfather died. Joe Watson entered the hospital in January of 2003, seeking treatment for congestive heart failure. He was a very sick man. The last Friday he was in the hospital, Joe repeatedly remarked that he wanted to go home. His family naturally assumed he wanted to leave the hospital and return to the home he and his wife shared. Later, they realized Joe was readying himself to go to his heavenly home. Somehow, he must have known his death was imminent

April intended to go to the hospital to see her grandfather over the weekend; however, Joe died suddenly before dawn on Saturday morning before she got the chance. April felt terrible about not being able to see Joe before he died. She was sad that she did not get to say goodbye.

Several days after the funeral, April stayed up late one night cleaning her house while her husband and boys slept. As she worked, April talked to her grandfather quietly even though she knew he was gone. She asked him to forgive her for not getting to the hospital in time to see him before he passed away.

Walking from the kitchen to the living room, April stopped abruptly! There in the entryway of her home stood her deceased grandfather, Joe. Joe looked vibrant and much younger than he was at the time he died and he smiled broadly at April. She noticed he was standing up tall and straight, not stooped over, as he had been later in life. Joe did not speak words. There was really no need for words! The fact that April could see her deceased grandfather standing in her home was an incredible experience for her!

His presence conveyed joy and peace to April. She did not attempt to speak to him. Joe did not linger long and when he was certain that April had seen him, he faded out of sight. April felt as if an angel had touched her! She missed her grandfather after that encounter but she no longer felt guilt. Instead, she felt a peaceful assurance that all was well and her grandfather was safely home in Heaven.

PART 2

April's grandmother, Jessie Watson, died in December of 2010 in McMinnville, Tennessee, from heart failure. She died one week before Christmas. In life, Mrs. Watson shared her faith, her kindness, and her generosity with family members and friends. Everyone loved Mrs. Watson! April lived beside her grandmother most of her life and the two of them were very close.

Soon after Mrs. Watson died, April got out of bed one night to check on her young son, Eli. She noticed a light was on in the dining room. She discovered one light was glowing from the chandelier. That little light being on was very strange because the chandelier had never been connected to an electrical source. It was not functional; it was for looks only. April recalled her grandmother's familiar habit of keeping a night light on every night. She did not see her grandmother at that time but she felt strongly the light incident was in some way related to her deceased grandmother.

Each individual light on the chandelier could work independently of each other. In order to make one light work, someone had to climb a ladder to remove the candlestick from the chandelier, twist the connecting battery end, then replace the candle back in the base. No one in April's house caused the light to turn on. One week later, the same light turned on again with no human assistance.

April found the incident very comforting and was convinced her grandmother came to say goodbye and used the night light to make her presence known. In the months that followed, April repeatedly heard noises coming from the dining room when no one was in that room. The noise was a creaking noise, as if someone was walking around in that room. She did not hear the actual footsteps, only the noise that might have been the result of the weight of a person walking back and forth there. April attributed those noises to visitations from her deceased grandmother since there was no other logical explanation for the noises. She even recorded the noise on one occasion. The noises stopped after that.

Mrs. Watson had a strong affinity for red birds! Her family placed a lovely red bird in her funeral floral arrangement because they were all aware of her affection for them. Soon after the funeral, April became the recipient of numerous red bird visits. The first red bird appeared in a tree next to her patio. Snow fell the night before and when April opened her window blinds the next morning, she saw a gorgeous red bird perched on the snowy bough of the tree, looking at her. She felt certain that God sent the bird as a sign, to remind her that her grandmother was safely in His care.

From then on, the red bird became a part of April's life. She has seen the two-legged winged animal in times of trouble, sickness, and sadness in various locations, at home and away from home.

Eli, April's young son, asked one day, "Mom, why did we never see red birds before Grandma died?"

April acknowledged that she did not recall seeing red birds before the funeral either and she replied, "It must be God's way of making us smile when we think of Grandma."

Chapter 23

TIFFANY

God is in control, and sometimes He overrules our decisions to remind us of that. Divine intervention is God's way of carrying out His plan in our lives in spite of our plans. Dawn Jordan gave birth to her first son when she was 24 years old. Less than two years later, she gave birth to her second son. Dawn and her husband both agreed they only wanted two children, so before Dawn left the hospital they discussed their decision with her doctor.

A surgeon performed a tubal ligation on Dawn as a form of sterilization, a permanent form of birth control. The surgeon cut each fallopian tube, severing each tube into two separate parts. He then tied off each end of each severed fallopian tube. As a final precaution, the doctor cauterized (burned) the ends of the fallopian tubes. That procedure was the real deal and it ended Dawn's childbearing days.

Dawn left the hospital with her new baby boy and she felt quite confident about their decision. She was relieved after having the surgical procedure. After only days at home, Dawn felt like she had twins because the child that was under two years old was still a baby. She had two babies, just different sized babies!

Eight months later, Dawn found herself struggling to care for her two small boys. In the days that followed, Dawn felt sick. She felt weak and tired and nauseated on a daily basis. Each day, the nausea grew more severe. She went to her doctor who gave her medication for a suspected virus. Dawn took the medication and she did not get better.

A couple of weeks passed and Dawn went back to her doctor because she knew she was seriously ill. She thought she might even be dying! Her symptoms were that bad. The doctor took blood samples and did some routine tests. Two days later, Dawn's doctor called and informed her she was 16 to 18 weeks pregnant. Dawn refused to believe that incredulous report until she had an ultrasound and actually heard the baby's heart beat.

The following January, Dawn gave birth to a perfectly adorable baby girl and they named her Tiffany! She was beautiful and perfect in every way. Dawn set out to raise her three babies to the best of her abilities, even though they made her feel like she had triplets at times! There were days when all the babies cried at the same time and Dawn sat on the floor and cried with them sometimes!

One day, Dawn looked in her jewelry box and spotted the mothers ring she had received as a Christmas gift before they knew about the bonus baby girl. She picked up the ring and made a startling discovery. Three gemstones adorned the top of the ring band. The first was a ruby for her son's July birth, the third was an amethyst for her other son's February birth and the center stone was a garnet. Dawn and her husband shared January birthdays and they decided to put one stone in the center that represented their birth month because the ring did not look right with only two gemstones.

Dawn smiled and nodded her head in acknowledgement as she looked up to Heaven. Tiffany's birth month gemstone was a garnet since she was born in January too. The ring had been created long before Tiffany was born and it was perfect, needing no modification. Tiffany was part of God's plan and the mother's ring confirmed that to Dawn. Dawn's faith came into being when she gave birth to her miracle baby girl!

That day, Dawn prayed a simple prayer, "Dear God, I understand now. There are no accidents where You are concerned. You are in control. I understand that now, Lord, and I thank You for my little girl."

Chapter 24

NALIAH'S VISIT

The morning of June 28, 2007, began normally for Renee Schultz in West Allis, Wisconsin. Renee scurried about doing house-cleaning chores and preparing food for the children. Nathan was seven, Naomie was six, and Naliah was only three years old. Renee's mom reminded her of the church party they were supposed to attend that afternoon. It was to be a small gathering of preschool children having lots of food, games, and summer fun!

Renee and the kids arrived at the party and the fun began. The children were all very excited and they darted in all directions. Some of them splashed around climbing in and out of the swimming pool! A few of the little ones played on the swings. Naliah climbed onto a swing and Renee pushed the swing higher and higher as Naliah squealed with delight! Her laughter filled the air with pure happiness!

Renee froze in her tracks when she heard her deceased father's voice speaking to her, clearly and concisely. He spoke, saying Naliah was going to die that very day. Renee could hardly breathe as she stood motionless staring into space. She quickly told herself, "Naliah will not die today. She is here with her friends and she is having fun."

Just minutes later, Renee heard panic in a little girl's voice as the child screamed, saying someone was at the bottom of the pool. Renee felt dread rising up inside her and she began screaming Naliah's name repeatedly. She ran and jumped into the pool! Naliah's little body lay motionless at the bottom of the pool. Renee carried Naliah to the edge of the pool and placed her body flat on the ground. Renee's heart broke as she stroked Naliah's hair and gently closed her eyes with her fingertips. She did not want to believe all the life was gone from her little angel, Naliah, but that was the case. Renee heard her own voice saying to Naliah, "You have to go be with God now." She felt as if she was trapped in a dream.

After some time, Renee managed to stand up. She told herself she had to accept God's will. Renee knew it was time to say goodbye to her daughter, at least for the time being.

Renee's church conducted a special mass later that night. When it was over, Renee went home and collapsed into a deep sleep. From the darkness, invisible hands lifted Renee to a place where she entered a peaceful, dream-like state; she heard herself praying as she ascended. She saw what appeared to be the back seat of a car and a voice asked her to sit there and wait. Next, she heard Naliah's familiar sweet voice calling her name, and then she felt Naliah's precious little arms hugging her tightly! Renee awoke after that and she experienced a strong feeling of relief. Renee did not understand what she experienced or where she was when she visited her daughter, but she was grateful she had the opportunity to say goodbye to Naliah!

Three days later, Renee reached a point where she felt drained of all emotion and she needed to escape into the oblivion of sleep. Once again, there in the darkness, Renee felt herself ascending into the familiar dream-like state. Like before, she heard Naliah's sweet voice calling her name. Naliah touched her mom's cheek with her fingers to comfort her. Renee looked to her right and she saw Naliah slowly walking with an angel wearing white clothing. Naliah and the angel slowly walked away and entered into a consuming tunnel of brilliant white light until they became one with the light! Renee said goodbye and released Naliah into God's hands. Renee awoke with confidence and a peace that God had Naliah in His care.

Chapter 25

Nancy Bush and Martha Binns' Experiences

Part 1

Nancy Bush was only 12 years old when she became severely ill with rheumatic fever. A short time after she received the diagnosis, Nancy's doctor administered an injection of penicillin as part of her treatment. Nancy had never had the drug before, so her parents had no way of knowing she was allergic to it. An allergic reaction to penicillin sent Nancy into an unconscious state at once.

In an instant, Nancy found herself floating at ceiling level above her own body! She watched the doctor working to administer drugs to counteract the effects of the drug in an effort to save her life. The child felt very strange as she floated in midair, able to observe the scene below. She was aware that something unusual was happening; however, she never felt fear or anxiety. The experience was a pleasant one and it amused the child. It lasted for a very brief time.

Nancy did return to her body but she had full recall of what happened during her *near-death experience*. She holds dear the sense of peace and tranquility that surrounded her during that transitory excursion outside her earthly shell!

PART 2

Decades later, Nancy Bush and her mom enjoyed a delicious breakfast at a restaurant before they drove back to Nancy's home in Hermitage, Tennessee. Nancy got out of the car and walked toward her kitchen door. She heard her mom, Elise, calling to her. Elise asked Nancy to "come quickly" back to the car. Nancy's mother had picked up her cell phone to call her husband and she discovered the phone was in use. As soon as her eyes looked at the phone screen, she noticed the phone was independently calling the number of her deceased daughter, Martha. There was no answer, because 61-year-old Martha died two weeks earlier. Elise heard the cell phone ringing when she placed it to her ear and the ringing ended only when she forced the phone to end the call.

Nancy and her mom were not quite sure what to make of the call. They knew the call was no accident and they both felt relief when they reflected on the incident. Nancy and Elise reached the same conclusion. They believed that Martha had sent them a message, by way of an *after-death call*, letting them know she was all right!

PART 3

The next incident happened about one month after Martha Binns died of pancreatic cancer. Martha's sister, Nancy Bush, was soundly asleep one September morning in 2003. Nancy remembered that she felt helpless and unable to rouse herself from a deep, deep sleep that shrouded her. Suddenly, Nancy's deceased sister Martha appeared next to her bed. Her body appeared as mist except for her hair. Her hair was shiny and beautiful as it was at the time of her death. Her hair was a mixture of black and white hair, a salt and pepper mix. Nancy perceived Martha as a being full of peace and love. Nancy initially experienced the *after-death appearance* while she was still asleep but vividly got a glimpse of Martha as soon as she became fully awake.

Martha stood near the bed and she spoke forcefully to her sister, Nancy, saying, "Wake up Nancy, wake up!" Her voice was clear and decisive and Nancy felt certain that Martha came because she sensed she was in trouble waking up from an unnatural sleep. Nancy believed Martha saved her life. Nancy remains hopeful today that her sister will always be her guardian angel! Nancy was comforted by the fact that someone who loved her was watching over her.

Chapter 26

A MOTHER'S MESSAGES

J amie Holt of Wheeling, West Virginia struggled with the loss of her mom. Rita Smith passed away just two days after she turned 65. Jamie's son, Jackson, was three and her daughter, Jenna, was only six weeks old at the time. Jamie wished Rita had lived longer so she could have known Jenna and Jack the way she knew her older grandchildren. She felt sad because death robbed her children of the love of a very special grandmother.

Jamie, Jenna, and Jack visited her mom a short time before she died. Jamie was in the kitchen preparing lunch for all of them when she overheard her mom talking to the kids. Rita spoke softly to Jenna, saying, "Little girl, I wish I could watch you grow up. I will watch you from Heaven. I will be watching over all my grandbabies from Heaven." Rita died a few weeks later.

One afternoon, several weeks after the funeral, Jamie sat at her desk working diligently. She experienced a strong impulse to call her babysitter and check on three-year-old Jack. She ignored the feeling and continued working until she heard a clearly audible voice speaking directly into her ear! Jamie heard her deceased mom's voice forcefully and urgently speaking one word. "Jack!"

Jamie immediately picked up the phone and called the sitter who answered on the first ring. Little Jack was crying loudly and sounded frightened for no apparent reason. He was obviously having a bad day.

Jamie had the sitter place the phone to Jack's ear and she talked to him, calming him down as only a momma can do. The day would come when Jamie would look back on that afternoon as a trial run. *Her mom needed her to learn to listen and respond to her voice!*

Two years later, Jamie took her children to visit her dad. Mindy, Jamie's sister, and her two daughters accompanied them for the visit. Don Timbrook, Jamie's dad, lived in a rural community near Triadelphia, West Virginia. His property was adjacent to two farms. A fence separated grazing cattle from their playful children who watched with youthful curiosity and enthusiasm! The warm sunshine on that early spring day enticed the children to linger in the backyard. Jamie saw no harm in allowing two-year-old Jenna to remain outside under the watchful eyes of her nieces, Hannah and Brooke, who were ages 11 and 8. The moms instructed the kids to play in the secluded safety of the backyard only.

Jamie and Mindy retreated to the kitchen where they could talk, keeping a close eye on the children through a rear window. Jamie and Mindy were deep in conversation when Jamie experienced "the feeling." It was the feeling she had the day she called the babysitter when Jack needed her!

Suddenly, Jamie heard her mom's voice firmly commanding her to "*Get the girls!*" Jamie sprang to her feet while Mindy was in mid-sentence! One look toward the empty backyard filled Jamie with dread. Jamie ran to the front of the house as fast as she could go. Mindy ran after Jamie asking what was wrong.

The door slammed behind them as Jamie's feet landed on slippery ground in front of the house. The ground was still muddy and saturated from heavy rainfall that lasted several days prior to that day. In horror, Jamie and Mindy saw the girls covered in mud, walking on the main road where there was no shoulder to walk on. The distance between them was too great and going on foot would not get the kids to safety in time. A car sped past them, veering into the far lane to avoid striking the little three-some. Jamie yelled loudly, "Get off the road!"

The children had wandered away to see the donkeys grazing at the fence near the front of the property. The yard in front of the house was elevated and dropped off sharply leading straight down to the edge of the pavement. The girls got too close to the edge and were unable to maintain footing. The wet soil simply gave way beneath them and they slid into harm's way. They found it impossible to climb back up the way they came down and the only way out was to walk down the road toward the driveway in the path of moving traffic.

Jamie's mind raced and she reacted with precision. The moms jumped into Jamie's van and sped down the driveway and onto the road. Mindy pulled the frightened, soaking-wet, muddy kids into the van and Jamie drove them to safety! It only took a minute to pull them inside but it seemed like two hours!

The family was emotional and shaken as they rode back to the house. Mindy scolded her young daughters for making a poor decision, all the while knowing they were blessed to be alive! Jamie cried when she began to comprehend what really happened. Mindy wanted to know why Jamie ran to the front yard and how she knew something was wrong. Jamie replied, "Mom was watching them. She made me understand they were in trouble. She told me to 'get the girls.' Mom may have just saved their lives."

"I heard my mother's voice as plain as day," Jamie said. "She spoke my son's name into my ear the day he was at the sitter's house. I knew I needed to call the sitter that day. I heard my mother's voice a second time when she warned me my children were in danger. Three words made me jump to my feet and run!"

"There was a time when I worried because Mom would never know Jack and Jenna. Now I have peace in my heart. I know Mom knows the children and is probably with them more now than she would have been if she were still here in her physical body. In Mom's final years, she was confined to a wheel chair. She is in Heaven and human limitations no longer restrain her. I believe my mother is able to see Jack playing soccer. I believe she can watch Jenna's dance recitals. I always wanted a sign that Mom was all right, and I got it!"

Chapter 27

STEPHEN BARD'S STORY

I n August of 2010, Stephen Bard was living a happy and successful life in Washington, DC. He was earning a great salary and he had all the material possessions anyone could hope to have. Stephen believed in Jesus and he prayed to God, usually when he had a need. Most of the time, he felt self-sufficient and he preferred taking care of his own affairs.

Stephen lost his mom that summer because of complications arising from a barrage of health problems. Cancer, respiratory problems, and heart problems assaulted Donna Bard from the time she was 27 years old. Donna was a woman of great faith and her family received comfort from knowing she surely went to Heaven when she died. *Stephen would never have guessed how the loss of his mother would affect him in the months that followed!*

Three months after Donna died, Stephen's sister, Jill Beattie, called Stephen and encouraged him to consider moving back home to Shippensburg, Pennsylvania, to take care of his dad. That was a life-changing decision. Going from busy independent living in Washington, DC back to his childhood home in the role of a caregiver was life-changing.

As soon as Stephen arrived in Pennsylvania, he began searching for a job. He was surprised when his search turned up only two employment possibilities for which he was qualified. The first one was a position working for a large book publishing company as a sales representative. The publisher was a large Christian publishing company. That job would afford him the ability to work with Christian authors and bookstores all across the country. The second option was for a management position in an adult bookstore. That job would afford him the ability to work with people who were less likely to be Christians. His job would be selling products that adversely affected the very souls of his customers.

Stephen told himself, "This is no coincidence! I can go to work for the Lord or for the devil." He felt he was being tested to see if he would choose good over evil. Stephen moved quickly and the Christian publishing company hired him. His past work history clearly indicated everything he had done so far had shaped and molded him for working in the publishing industry. *Stephen sensed a strong force pulling him in a predetermined direction.*

Enthusiasm filled Stephen each day when he began working at his new job! On the home front, Stephen's dad grew more distressed and anguished each day. Stephen found it increasingly difficult to deal with all the memories in his childhood home without his mother. Donna Bard had been a pillar of strength to her family and her absence became less bearable as time went by. Each day of Stephen's life was like a roller coaster ride, filled with highs at work and lows at home!

The people Stephen worked with had no knowledge of his mother's death or his home life situation. He struggled to focus and was not able to do the job he knew he was capable of doing. Weeks passed and feelings of hopelessness and despair steadily crept into Stephen's mind. He struggled to smile and fought the urge to sit down and cry many days. The intensity of the distressing mental anguish confused Stephen. Stephen experienced inner turmoil that led to exasperation. This genuinely caring man found himself caught up in an emotional and spiritual tug of war.

Stephen engaged in several conversations with a client who lived in Mount Vernon, Missouri in his early days at the publishing house. The man was known as the Rambling Rabbi and Stephen knew him as Rabbi Eukel. They always talked about books and the rabbi's radio show but never about Stephen's personal life. Stephen managed to keep everyone thinking all was well in his world!

Something happened on March 14, 2011, that greatly affected his relationship with the Lord! That day was the second worst day of his life since his mother passed away. The night before, for the first time, Stephen had a vivid dream about his mom. In the dream, his mom walked up to him, kissed him on the cheek, and told him she loved him. He woke up somewhat startled. The dark stillness coupled with the reality that his mom was gone left Stephen feeling brokenhearted.

Stephen prayed to God in earnest, asking Him to take away the extreme pain and distress. He realized he could not endure one more day without help and he asked God to do something to make things better; he was desperate! Soon Stephen fell back asleep and dreamed the same dream a second and a third time! He was convinced his mom had paid him three distinct visits in the night. Stephen awoke before daylight in a great deal of emotional pain. He petitioned the Lord for help only God could give to end the unbearable suffering.

Stephen worked out at the gym that morning before arriving at work heavy-hearted, empty, and confused. Soon after he settled into his work routine, he received a call from Rabbi Eukel. Automatically, Stephen snapped into his performance role as the enthusiastic salesman and answered with, "Gooooood morning, Rabbi Eukel!"

He replied, "Shalom, Stephen, and how are you today?"

Stephen answered, "Wonderful, Rabbi, what can I do for you today?"

"Well, I'm not really sure," replied the Rabbi. "I'm sitting here with my wife in a doctor's office. I noticed a book published by your company on the table in the waiting room. I took one look at the book and I heard God's voice speaking clearly to me. He said I was to call you, Stephen, because you are having a very hard day. God told me that I was to pray for you this morning."

All the pent-up emotions inside Stephen suddenly dissolved as tears trickled silently down his face. The sadness melted away and pure joy filled the empty place inside him. Stephen knew God had heard and answered his prayer! He was convinced beyond doubt that God was speaking directly to him through a stranger who had no earthly knowledge about him. The rabbi had no way of knowing about Stephen's inner turmoil or his painful situation. Only God could have caused Rabbi Eukel to call *on that particular day, at that specific time, after that desperate prayer for emotional healing!*

When the phone call ended, Stephen was elated because the pain and despair was gone! He was completely aware that healing and restoration had filled him supernaturally, straight from Heaven! God changed Stephen from that moment on! The fact that God spoke to him through a stranger, whom he had never personally met, was the defining moment!

"If someone at work had seen my anguish and offered to pray for me, I would not have believed that was God talking to me. I could not deny it was God speaking to me when a man whom I had never met called me from across the country, unexpectedly, offering to pray for me out of obedience to God's instruction.

"Until that day, I was a skeptic that God would speak to an ordinary person like me. I am just one grain of sand in the universe. Now I know with all certainty that God did talk to me that day through Rabbi Eukel. The peace of God filled me up! It was unlike anything I had ever experienced. I know now, God really is with me every minute of the day and night," Stephen said.

Stephen said, "I use to think success was measured by how much I earned, the people I knew, and what I owned. When Mother passed away, none of that mattered to me anymore. When you leave this life, you take nothing with you except your faith in God and the certainty of Heaven. I finally understand the only thing that matters is knowing Jesus Christ as Savior. He gave me perfect peace and God is caring for my mom right now! My Heavenly Father brought my heart home again to Him and to my family."

Chapter 28

CARMINE'S AFTER-DEATH SIGNS TO JO ANN

C armine Colabro departed this life on May 20, 2010, in Gallatin, Tennessee, after an 11-year battle with Alzheimer's disease. Carmine's wife, Jo Ann Colabro, and daughter Vicky stood by his bedside as his life ended.

In the minutes that followed, Jo Ann sat rubbing Carmine's arm as she told him good-bye. A small perfect cross, approximately one inch tall, appeared on Carmine's right inner arm, just above the elbow. Jo Ann got very excited when she saw it and she directed Vicky's attention to it. Carmine's caregiver, Tia, saw the cross and the three of them agreed they had never seen anything like it. The cross appeared during the dying process, for it was not there earlier in the day.

When the hospice nurse arrived, the cross had vanished. Three witnesses saw the death mark and each person described it in the same way. Jo Ann received it as a confirmation that Carmine had reached Heaven; that all was well.

Two days passed and Jo Ann was home alone, going through photographs in preparation for the funeral display. Suddenly, she heard a loud racket and it sounded like something came through the kitchen ceiling! Jo Ann went to the kitchen in search of the cause of the disturbing noise. Beside the breakfast bar, Carmine's sword collection was stored in a wooden rack. Two of the long swords lay on the floor beside the bar. There was no explanation for why the swords were out of the rack and on the floor. Jo Ann was puzzled and she placed the swords back in the rack.

The following day, Jo Ann heard the same loud crashing noise and returned to the kitchen to find the same swords were out of the rack and on the floor again. There was no logical explanation for the sword displacement because Jo Ann was alone in the house. That did not happen a third time.

Carmine's daughter and son-in-law arrived later that morning from Cleveland, Ohio. After they arrived, Jo Ann searched for Carmine's obituary online and as soon as she did, the song called Ava Maria began wafting from the computer speakers. Carmine had always been very fond of that song! Jo Ann attempted to exit the website; however, the music kept right on playing. All her attempts to silence the music were futile and the music continued until late afternoon, at which time it stopped as suddenly as it began.

Jo Ann and Carmine's daughter, Corrine, sat together engrossed in a conversation later that same day when the two of them heard an extremely loud crash in Carmine's office. A search revealed a wall shelf had been lifted out of the brackets that supported and secured it, causing it to fall to the floor. Corrine spoke aloud saying, "All right, Dad, we know you are here!"

Corrine's husband, Jeff, came in to reposition the shelf and he commented that he saw no way the shelf could have fallen. He said the shelf had to be lifted from below and pushed upward to dislodge it, allowing it to fall.

Jo Ann was not surprised by all the commotion because she and Carmine had discussed his death. He had a strong desire to let her know he was all right when he crossed over from this life to Heaven.

In the following months, Corrine and others witnessed lights going on when no one flipped the switch. She also witnessed Carmine's lift chair operating all by itself with no human help. Carmine did not like this chair. He told Jo Ann to take it back and get the money back, because he could not learn how to use the remote for the chair. Jo Ann stood speechless as the lift chair activated and lifted the seat to the highest position possible. Jo Ann felt like Carmine was letting her know, "Hey, I can operate this thing now!"

During an illness, while Jo Ann lay sick in bed, she heard footsteps in the house. She was alone in the house and she knew it had to be Carmine, so she just laid there, face down. The footsteps came into the bedroom and she felt a hand patting her on the head as one soothes a sick child. She felt the hairs on her arm standing on end. She never opened her eyes because she was afraid she would not be able to see him, or she would be bothered by the way he looked. Later on, she wished she had looked.

Soon after that, Jo Ann saw Carmine's shadow on the bathroom door as she walked toward it. She did not know what to do so she started talking to Carmine and she demonstrated no fear. She tried to assure him that she would be all right without him. The shadow vanished and that is when the supernatural visits ended. Jo Ann felt a sense of relief at that time and she felt sure that Carmine was at peace in his heavenly home.

Chapter 29

Uncle Tom's Healing Visit

Victoria Watkins[1] observed her Aunt Louise and Uncle Tom in the hospital room at St. Thomas Hospital in Nashville, Tennessee. She had a hard time believing that Aunt Louise could go from being strong, vivacious, and active to bed-ridden and dying so quickly. It all happened so fast and the cancer in her lungs progressed, quickly draining the life out of the woman Victoria loved so dearly.

Victoria's aunt faced death with courage and her regret was for those loved ones she was leaving behind, not herself. She was a strong Christian and she did not doubt that she would soon be in that perfect place called Heaven. As her time of departure drew near, Louise focused on one issue that weighed heavily on her mind. She felt like she simply could not leave this earth until she was sure that her husband, Tom, had accepted Jesus as his Savior. As a dying woman, she made only one request and her Tom agreed to honor that request.

Louise's pastor stood near the hospital bed as he led Tom in a simple prayer. Tom prayed after the pastor and he prayed for forgiveness of his sins, he repented or "turned away" from his old life and asked Jesus Christ to come into his heart as Lord and Savior. God supernaturally changed Tom at that moment and Tom's decision and conscious act changed his eternal destination from hell to Heaven.

Louise was very happy at that moment because she knew she would see Tom again in Heaven. All because of the decision he just made and the prayer he just prayed. A short time later, Louise passed away quietly, leaving behind her husband and their only adult child, Katie.

Five months later, Victoria accompanied her cousin Katie to Tom's home when Katie was unable to reach him by phone. The two women entered the home searching in opposite ends of the house. Victoria found Tom lying on the floor in the kitchen. He was dead from an apparent heart attack.

For many weeks after the funeral, Victoria had trouble sleeping at night. Her mind took her unwillingly back to that kitchen where she found Tom on the floor. She experienced night terrors and unusual symptoms in her body when she did finally sleep at all.

Repeatedly, she entered a deep-sleep state that gripped her in a powerful way until she felt like she was dying when she could not awaken. Her arms and legs turned ice cold, she felt numb and unable to move. Victoria's severely debilitating sleep episodes continued from the time of Tom's death in April until September. She was extremely perplexed about her condition and contemplated seeing a physician about the sleep abnormalities.

In September, Victoria awoke one night and to her amazement, she saw the deceased, Tom, in her bedroom. She looked up from where she lay and to the left side of the bed. He was actually positioned higher than if he had been standing on the floor. Tom looked down on Victoria and he patiently waited to speak. He gave her time to be clear-headed, then he spoke to her saying, "I am okay; I am well. I am no longer sick and I no longer have pain. Don't worry about me anymore; I am fine."

Tom wore a white shirt and jeans that night and his face looked very young and vibrant. He looked forty years younger than he was at the time of his death. His voice and expressions indicated he was truly at peace and he was happy!

Tom finished speaking. Slowly he faded from view, leaving Victoria in a state of wonder and awe at what she just witnessed. Her Uncle Tom had been right there with her seconds ago and he was very much alive although she attended his funeral several months ago!

After that night, Victoria's sleep patterns returned to normal. Good health returned to Victoria, she no longer dreaded nighttime, and she slept soundly from then on.

NOTE

1. This is a true story, but the names were changed to comply with a privacy request.

Chapter 30

A "MELODIE" OF LOVE

On July 27, 1962, Dorothy and William Orr of Barrington, New Jersey, rejoiced when Dorothy gave birth to their first daughter! Dorothy was a choral music teacher. It seemed fitting to name their daughter "Melodie." From the time Melodie was an infant, her mother and her maternal grandmother, Hannah, sang a hymn to Melodie. The hymn became Melodie's song since her name was in the lyric. Here are the words to part of the hymn:

> In my heart there rings a melody, rings a melody of Heaven's harmony,
>
> In my heart there rings a melody, rings a melody of love.
>
> I have a song that Jesus gave me, it was sent from Heaven above,
>
> There never was a sweeter melody, 'tis the melody of love.[1]

Dorothy and William were devoted Christians for their entire lives, and when Melodie was born, they were active in their Presbyterian Church. Dorothy served as organist and director of choirs, as well as in many other areas of church work. William was involved as an elder, deacon, and Sunday school teacher. Melodie grew up immersed in the life and teachings of the church. As an adult, Melodie served the church as a choir member, Sunday school teacher, elder, organizer, and teacher of the children's summer Bible school programs, and member of the United Presbyterian Women's Organization.

Melodie matured into a lovely red-haired woman with a quiet, kind, and gentle manner. She possessed a ready smile and was loved and respected by all who knew her. Sadness entered the lives of the Orr family in February of 1999, when Melodie's dad passed away. The family had a strong Christian background, so they weathered that storm by faith, knowing that death meant transition, not the end. On September 29, 2000, sadness struck again when Melodie came home from work not feeling well. She collapsed inside her mother's home and was rushed to Underwood Memorial Hospital in Woodbury, New Jersey. For several days, her mother, her sister, Carol, and devoted brother, William, and their families kept a vigil at her bedside. On October 1, 2000, Melodie's mom and a few close friends left the hospital briefly to get a meal before going back to be with Melodie .

At that point, Dorothy became caught up in a supernatural experience that surprised her greatly. Suddenly, she sensed Melodie's spiritual presence all around her! Mental telepathy is an accurate description of how she knew in her heart that Melodie had just died. Dorothy had clear knowledge and a simple understanding that Melodie had left her body and was no longer in that hospital bed. Dorothy began to process what just happened with her dear daughter. She felt certain that Melodie wanted to communicate with her regarding preferences for her own upcoming church funeral service.

Dorothy quickly grabbed a pen from her purse and a napkin from the restaurant table. Hastily, she wrote down all the precise details Melodie imparted to her. Melodie's favorite color was lavender, and she asked to have lavender colored flowers, plates, and napkins at the luncheon following her funeral service. More importantly, Melodie imparted the particular scripture she wanted the pastor to share at her funeral. It was Psalms 30:11, *"Thou has turned for me my mourning into dancing"* (KJV).

Dorothy was amazed and comforted at the same time at the end of the supernatural occurrence and certain interaction with her daughter in the minutes following her death transition. The comfort she received from the inexplicable experience was further confirmation of her already strong and steadfast Christian faith in a wonderful afterlife.

October 6, 2000, was the funeral date for the beautiful soul known as Melodie Jayne Orr. The service was at Christ Presbyterian Church in Gibbstown, New Jersey, the home church of the Orr family for the past 25 years. The beautiful church bulletins reflected the scripture verse of Melodie's own choosing. Lavender flower blossoms framed the words, *"Thou hast turned my mourning into dancing."* Dorothy was unbelievably strong and a vibrant Christian witness at the service. She stood up and asked everyone to clap their hands in praise for the Lord and Melodie's life during the first hymn. During the time of remembrance, Dorothy thanked friends and family for attending the service. She told the congregation that Melodie made a previous decision to be an organ donor. Her choice was characteristic of her 38 years of giving to others. Dorothy noted that Melodie would be pleased to know that her kidneys, liver, and the corneas of her eyes had already reached recipients, making three lives better!

Dorothy continued by sharing Melodie's after-death visit in the form of a supernatural experience to all the listeners to bless them the way she was blessed by it. She also told the touching story of singing, "In my heart there rings a melody" to Melodie from infancy.

Dorothy also encouraged everyone to use the circumstances as a time to strengthen his or her own personal walks with the Lord.

As the service ended, everyone placed a flower on the casket while singing Melodie's song, "Melody of Love." The tune remained in the air until the last flower adorned the casket lid in fond farewell.

Note: Dorothy's second daughter, Carol, was named for "Christmas carols" because she was born in December. Carol was a strong supporter for Dorothy in the years that followed. Dorothy passed away in her 75th year on earth. Carol visited her mom's vacant house after a Sunday church service several weeks later. She was there alone and feeling rather lonely when the strong, sweet fragrance of flowers filled the entire room! That struck Carol as odd, since no live flowers had been in the home for months. Carol could only surmise that Dorothy was conveying a "melody of love" to her through the fragrant essence of an invisible bouquet of flowers!

NOTE

1. Elton Menno Roth, "In My Heart, There Rings a Melody," 1924.

Chapter 31

A HEAVENLY EXPERIENCE

October 22, 2011 marked the third anniversary of the passing of Michael Tropiano, Andrea Toanone's father. She felt very sad when she awoke that morning in Woodbury, New Jersey, thinking about how much time had passed since she last saw her dad in earthly form. She was still lying in her bed when something very unusual happened. Initially, Andrea felt and heard simultaneously a powerful "swishing" sound! Intuitively she knew her soul was being swept upward and away from her body, that a transference of energy was taking place. She was about to take a voyage into eternity!

Andrea's out-of-body experience began at 11:00 A.M. and ended at 11:30 A.M. Andrea said her spirit and body separated and a force lifted her up in the air. She traveled into and through a powerful bright light, as bright as the sun! She found herself in a place she perceived to be Heaven, the Kingdom of God.

"I saw Jesus, who appeared to be ten feet tall, wearing a dazzling pure white robe. He smiled at me with tenderness and gave me a hug! Under his arms were my father in the middle, my Aunt Yolanda on the left, and my aunt Rita on the right. They had their arms around my dad. Dad spoke, saying he was proud of me and that he loved me dearly. He asked me to tell my mom, Joan, he loved her," Andrea said.

"I saw Aunt Nettie, Dad's sister-in-law, and she was wearing a black sequined dress. She asked me to tell Uncle Vince, Dad's brother, and their two children, Maria and Nicky, that she missed them and loved them. I also saw all of my four grandparents, wearing clothing of black and white. Both my grandmothers, Mary and Ella, wore old-fashioned 'Mary Jane' shoes and dresses from that same era. My grandfathers, Erich and Anthony, were similarly dressed in gray suits and tall hats. My maternal grandparents said to tell 'Joanie,' their daughter, that they love her. My Dad wore a gray suit, and then changed in a minute into his typical flannel blue and gray shirt with gray pants. My Mom's friend Dora was there too and sent her regards to Mom."

Andrea shared more details, saying, "People I had known on earth continued to appear before me and around me in that celestial setting. Eileen, mother of my brother-in-law Michael, appeared wearing a black dress and black necklace. She said, 'Tell Mikey-Mike and Linnie-Lin (her children) I love them!' My dad said to tell Michele (his daughter) and Katelin and Christopher (his grandchildren) that he loves them dearly. Others who appeared with messages for earthbound family members were Jack, my husband Hank's dad, wearing a gray suit and top hat, and Edith, Hank's grandmother. 'I love you' was the one common message that everyone there wanted to send back to loved ones here."

While Andrea was in Heaven, she saw winged angels flying and singing over streets of gold. She entered Heaven through a golden, pearly entrance gate adorned with various kinds of gemstones in colors of sapphire, teal, fuchsia, and lavender purple.

The Heavenly Father told Andrea to "Come into the Light!" When she entered the Light, she was awestruck by what she saw. It was Jesus on His throne surrounded by exquisite, pure, holy, radiant Light!

Andrea moved freely about in Heaven from one location to another in a constant state of wonder and amazement! She saw an incredible building that can only be described as a mansion. All the doors to the mansion had crosses on them and each door opened wide to reveal comfortable dwelling places filled with enough beds for even extended families to sleep on.

Vast fields of a variety of splendid and magnificent flowers surrounded the perimeter of the mansion. Andrea recalled seeing sunflowers and recognizable flowers like those on earth plus rare and beautiful flowers that she had never seen before. A glorious and gorgeous rainbow spanned the entire sky above!

Andrea saw the disciples of Jesus Christ there along with Mary, the Blessed Mother of Jesus. "It was grand sight, but almost too much to comprehend, seemingly like a holy apparition too marvelous to behold! There is a beautiful river in Heaven and everyone there is able to walk on water as well as land."

Andrea said, "The Tree of Life is located in the center of the Garden of Heaven. Magnificent peace was in and around everything and everyone; there was peace even in the precious sounds of the music I heard. The sounds of praise never stop in Heaven, and the music continually flows through the air like a sweet and gentle summer breeze. I heard three songs I can remember: 'In the Garden,' 'Amazing Grace,' and 'How Great Thou Art.' All songs were sung along with instruments, most memorably the harp, at the same time. The songs complimented each other, blending in perfect harmony, and pleasing precision."

Michael, Andrea's father, drew near to Andrea and he was holding luscious grapes in his hand. He smiled contentedly, offering some to Andrea, and then proceeded to eat some of them.

Andrea found herself perfectly content in that lovely celestial place of grandeur. She experienced indescribable peace and joy. Andrea was so pleased to be there with Jesus and her dad that she had no desire to leave. She noticed incomprehensible red and blue rays of suspended light radiating from Jesus' heart and chest area, just before He told her she had to go back to earth.

God the Father conveyed to Andrea that she had to return to earth to fulfill her purpose in life, which was to tell everyone about God and to make a difference in the lives of the students she taught. He instructed Andrea, "Pay attention to the 'signs,' and when you are called—*do My will*. I will work through you. You must instill the love of learning about Jesus in others, and then you will be ready to return to Heaven, to be with Me."

Andrea said after being in Heaven for thirty minutes (it seemed like eternity), her soul retracted into her human body and she was suddenly back on earth. She remembers much about Heaven and treasures each memory. She recalled, "I was myself there but in spiritual form. Our souls there are filled with the love of God and are illuminated by the light and glory of Jesus! I had wings and a halo above my head. I saw many others like me. We wore long robes of radiant, soft, white fabric, as Jesus wore."

She went on to say, "I now believe we have a cord that attaches our souls to our bodies to facilitate us when God allows us to leave earth and visit Heaven on rare occasions. I am amazed by the fact that Heaven visits are possible! I would not have believed it before I experienced that out-of-body journey.

"When we leave this body for the last time, then the cord will fail to retract and our souls separate from our bodies completely and ascend heavenward. I find it extremely comforting to know that as a child of God, saved by Jesus Christ, I can hold fast to the knowledge that I will be with Jesus and my loved ones one day. There I will enjoy the sweet peace and love of God forever."

> *Remember Him before the silver cord is broken and the golden bowl is crushed, the pitcher by the well is shattered and the wheel at the cistern is crushed; then the dust will return to the earth as it was, and the spirit will return to God who gave it* (Ecclesiastes 12:6-7).

Note from the author: I have heard of other stories similar to this one through research and through personal conversations with other highly-credible Christian witnesses. I find these personal accounts extremely encouraging!

Chapter 32

DIVINE COMFORT

D r. Michael Culbert was born in May of 1930 in the mountainous area of Molleystown, Pennsylvania. He graduated high school as Valedictorian in 1948. He attended college, earning his Bachelor of Science, Master's, and Doctoral degrees in the discipline of music. Dr. Culbert served in the military during the Korean War. He met his future wife, Esther, when she was only 16 years old and later married her. He spent most of his career at Clearview Regional High School in Mullica Hill, New Jersey, as a well-loved and creative instrumental music teacher and band director for 32 years.

Dr. and Mrs. Culbert were very athletic; the two of them and their family enjoyed many camping and hiking trips in almost every national park in the country. The two of them later backpacked the 2,100 mile Appalachian Trail that spans from Maine to Georgia. In 1995, at the age of 65, the duo bicycled 4,300 miles across the entire United States from Oregon to Virginia. After that, they toured Ireland and Scotland on their bikes. They also hiked in Wales and Scotland. Their adventures took them to Alaska, Canada, Europe, Scandinavia, Australia, New Zealand, Iceland, Costa Rica, and Panama.

Michael became a legend within his own circle of family, friends, and students. He served as a church organist and director of choirs for a span of 38 years, and continued to be very active in church life through his eightieth year. He touched the lives of countless youth, children, and adults in both his school and church positions in very positive ways through his love for God, family, and community.

On July 5, 2011, Dr. Michael Culbert suffered a stroke at his home in Sewell, New Jersey. An ambulance crew came to assist him and transported him to the hospital. Dr. Culbert's final journey was underway. From that day forward, he was never able to return to his beautiful, peaceful home surrounded by wildlife and trees. It was his home for 52 years, the place he had shared countless happy times with his wife and family. Dr. Culbert's daughter, Peggy Culbert, had several unusual experiences during those heart-wrenching weeks and months of change. *Each experience served as an affirmation of God's presence and power in her life.*

The stroke affected Dr. Culbert's ability to give or receive communication, leaving him in a small, secluded world of his own. Peggy had a difficult time adapting to her dad's incapacitated state, and she became discouraged. On the night of July 10, 2011, *as Peggy slept, she became the recipient of a rare supernatural manifestation of a presence that engulfed her entire body.* The presence affected Peggy like a holy aura, surrounding her being, and in moments she recognized the presence was her dad! Peggy focused on the presence, and she was able to see her dad's smiling face. He was the way he was before the stroke, at his best! He expressed his earnest desire to protect, love, and care for his daughter before he disappeared. Dr. Culbert did not speak with his mouth, but he imparted a message to Peggy. He expressed to her, "Be calm; everything will be fine. Have no fears." The extraordinary experience comforted Peggy greatly!

On August 25, 2011, Peggy drove her usual forty-minute route to work at an elementary school south of her home. She planned to ready her classroom in preparation for the new school year that began in September. By that time, her dad was experiencing his fourth move following the initial hospitalization to a rehabilitation center. The entire ordeal had taken a toll on Dr. Culbert, Esther, and Peggy.

Peggy made every conscious effort to keep her spirit strong. She surrounded herself with the things of God; she prayed and listened to uplifting music. Still, Peggy's concern grew for her mom who suffered from deep anguish about the ongoing circumstances over which she had no control. Dr. Culbert and his wife Esther were intertwined in each other's lives even now, at the ages of 80 and 81.

Peggy realized her immediate situation had not escaped God's attention and she knew it was a fine time to walk by faith and *prove* the power of faith. She began to trust God, expecting Him to evidence His presence to her in uncommon ways. Before the wonderful faith experiment was over, God revealed Himself to Peggy in *four separate messages* in one day! Peggy was extremely appreciative and she knew the messages were gifts from her Heavenly Father.

The first message appeared as Peggy drove toward her workplace. A huge truck traveled ahead of Peggy and she focused on the words written on the back of the truck trailer. It was a Bible passage from Romans 8:31. She could hardly stop smiling when she read, *"If God be for us, who can be against us?"* (KJV).

The second message appeared when Peggy drove to a convenience store to buy a couple of items. She parked her car facing the highway. Just before she drove out of the parking lot, a truck passed by her. To Peggy's surprise, she saw encouraging words displayed on the side of the trailer in large print. She read, *"In God We Trust."*

Peggy was quite pleased by the messages she accepted by faith as divine messages! She arrived at the school and completed her work, then headed home by a different route. She planned to stop at the rehabilitation facility to visit her dad on the way home. The third message of the day also appeared on the back of a large trailer of a big truck. Peggy could hardly believe it when she read the words, *"Praise the Lord!"* At that moment, Peggy began literally praising the Lord aloud in her car! She clearly understood that *God was communicating with her* in ways that only He could have orchestrated at precisely the right moments!

Peggy visited with her dad a while, then departed for home, traveling on Chapel Heights Road. She smiled, receiving yet another encouraging word from the road sign. She took it to mean, *"We can reach wonderful heights through chapel (God) worship!"* While Peggy was still smiling with a grateful heart, she drove past a church and noticed the words on a marquis. *"Come unto Me all ye that labor and are heavy laden, and I will give you rest,"* from Matthew 11:28 (KJV).

Peggy said, "It was like receiving a letter from God saying all the right things to lift a heavy heart to His way of thinking! God is an understanding Father, knowing that His children need to see Him sky-write words at times to sustain us in times of turmoil, and He is willing to provide in astonishing ways!" Peggy's faith experiment worked extremely well that day.

On Sunday, March 25, 2012, Dr. Culbert went home to Heaven at the age of 81. His family—wife Esther, daughter Peggy, sons James and Edward, two daughter-in-laws, and six grandchildren—took comfort in the fact that at the time of his passing at 11:50 A.M., his church congregation was singing "Lift High the Cross" as the concluding hymn of their worship service. In addition, the choral anthem that day was "Surely He Has Borne Our Grief and Carried Our Sorrows" (Isaiah 53:4), which also comforted the family.

In the days following her dad's passing, Peggy felt very sure in her spirit that she would receive a Divine supernatural sign or manifestation from Him *if she asked God with all her heart for it.* In this instance, however, she refrained from asking. She felt as if God had given her so many affirmations and confirmations throughout the prior year that it would almost seem as if she was ungrateful for blessings received if she asked for more. A bit reluctantly, she resigned to "leaving well enough alone."

Then, three days after her dad's passing, she received a special surprise! Her good spiritual friend, Denise Ibbotson, reported to her that as she was typing a letter of condolence to Peggy that day regarding Dr. Culbert's passing, *she experienced a clear vision manifestation of him!* Denise recognized him since she had met him briefly several times in the years prior to his passing. The deceased Dr. Culbert appeared to Denise *along with her own father* who had passed away many years prior to this time. The two men had never known each other on earth, but had apparently become acquainted in Heaven, knowing that their daughters were close spiritual friends.

Denise wrote, "I can literally see our dads becoming friends as I am writing this, and the two of them talking about their daughters to one another. They are smiling (beaming!) and proud and so happy that we share a friendship here. There is bright light all around them."

Peggy was so comforted. The "smiling" and "beaming" part of Denise's vision was important to her. Denise did not know Dr. Culbert sufficiently to realize that his smile was his trademark. Peggy knew, however, that throughout his entire life, Dr. Culbert was perhaps best known for his radiant smile, making Denise's vision affect her powerfully.

Dr. Culbert's funeral was scheduled for three days after that day, and Peggy felt led to play the piano and speak at the service. Her friend's divine vision of comfort fortified Peggy in a big way! She was able to participate in the funeral as planned, armed with a supernatural "blessed assurance" that the world cannot give!

One month passed, and then Peggy received one more very special divine surprise! Another good spiritual friend, Andrea Toanone, called her excitedly to report that *she had an after-death visit from Dr. Culbert* on May 3, 2012. Andrea reported that she had felt very ill that day and was becoming very concerned about a disconcerting unresolved health issue. In the midst of this, *Andrea experienced a profound vision manifestation where she saw the deceased Dr. Culbert along with her own deceased father.* Andrea, like Denise, had met Dr. Culbert briefly on several occasions in the years prior, and recognized him instantly.

Andrea was convinced that her own dad appeared to comfort and reassure her about her own condition and that Dr. Culbert appeared to her because he knew Andrea and Peggy were very close friends. He apparently knew that Andrea would share the details of the visit with his beloved daughter, Peggy.

Andrea's deceased dad appeared first, saying, *"Nothing is impossible with God!"* Next, the two dads, both whose first names were Michael, appeared together, each with an arm draped over the other one's shoulder. *Jesus appeared with them, surrounding them with His mighty arms of love!* The two Michaels said they were happy to meet each other for the first time in Heaven, and expressed how proud they were of their daughters.

The deceased Dr. Culbert said to Andrea, "Tell Peggy how proud I am of her and how thankful I am for all that she did to help Esther and me. Please tell her to be happy and enjoy life."

When the experience was over, Andrea scrambled for a pen to write down the communication before she forgot any of it. She grabbed the first thing she could find to write down the words. It was a free catalog she received from a store a short time before.

Andrea felt led to write the communication on a page next to a page bearing the likeness of broadly smiling Mickey Mouse with his arms open wide. He looked like he was made of crystal and he had a beautiful otherworldly appearance. When Andrea conveyed the experience to Peggy, she asked her if Mickey Mouse had a special meaning to Dr. Culbert, seeing the notes written next to his likeness.

Peggy exclaimed, "Yes!" Dr. Culbert grew up in the mountains of Schuylkill County, Pennsylvania, until the age of 18, when he went away to college. From the time he was born, everyone there called him "Mickey," short for Michael. He and his sister, Dawn, had matching plates with "Mickey and Minnie Mouse" on the center of the plates, which they had received as gifts in early childhood. Both had kept those plates as treasured items, even to the present time when both siblings were in their eighth decades of life. Dr. Culbert's relatives from the mountains never ceased calling him "Mickey." Peggy was amazed once more by God's power, wonderful "coincidences," and affirmations!

Peggy concluded, "The clear supernatural manifestations of God's presence and power were a wonderful divine comfort to me during this difficult time beginning in July of 2011. At that time, dad changed dramatically after being an unusually strong, healthy, intelligent, and multi-talented man for an extraordinary eighty years. I believe that his transition served as a healing for him and that he is presently happy, healthy, and active at his new residence in Heaven. I look forward to joyously meeting him again on the day that God chooses to call me Home!"

Chapter 33

SLOW MOTION

When I was a little girl growing up in rural Mississippi, I was involved in a very serious car accident. At the age of 10, I was assigned the chore of grocery shopping one Saturday morning. At that early age, I knew what to buy and what not to buy, and I made no exceptions! We had very little money. My father died at the age of 25, leaving three children under the age of five to be cared for by my mother. We did not own a car and town was two miles away. Mama seized the opportunity when the landowner where we lived and worked offered me a ride that morning.

I rode in the back seat of Mr. Landrum's new Plymouth, and I don't remember saying a word on the trip to town. My list was short and simple; I completed the shopping and placed the groceries in the trunk of the car for the ride home. My grandmother, who lived near us, rode in the back seat with me, and a cousin rode on the front seat with Mr. Landrum.

Central Mississippi is mostly flat land; however, there was a hill on the outskirts of town to the north. We began our descent down that hill, and something frightening happened. The car swerved from one side of the road to the other! I recall Mr. Landrum shouting, "I can't steer it! It won't stop!" The car careened from one shoulder of the road to the other as the car picked up speed going down the hill approaching the bridge that spanned Box's Creek. Strangely and fortunately, there were no other cars in sight at the moment.

There were no seat belts to restrain us, so we tossed from side to side as the car closed the distance between us and the bridge abutments of Box's Creek Bridge. The road was built up high to protect it from the creek overflow during heavy rains, and that elevation created an element of danger.

Just before we reached the bridge abutment, Mr. Landrum overcompensated and jerked the steering wheel hard to the left! We missed the bridge abutment and made a complete U-turn, which led us to the edge of the road where we began our descent. The car tumbled over and over and over until it came to rest against a row of trees and a barbed wire fence adjacent to a cotton field.

Divine intervention surely saved us! First, there were no cars in sight. Second, we did not hit the solid concrete bridge abutment. Third, we were not injured in the wreck. God's merciful power and angels filled that car, as real as the air we breathed! God left proof of His presence in the mind of a child. I remember how the car made a complete revolution several times, yet we did not crash against the glass or metal, as we logically should have. Somehow, God enclosed us in a safe place within the car, surrounded by more angels than I could count, in the form of sparkling particles of light!

From the moment we left the road, life changed! *We were in slow motion!* Inside the car on that particular day, we appeared to be weightless and *the laws of gravity no longer seemed to apply*. I felt no distress as my body tumbled in unison with the tumbling automobile! I was not injured when my head slowly impacted the ceiling of the car as it rolled over and over.

I distinctly remember seeing small sparkling particles of light floating before my curious eyes. They were everywhere, all around us! My mind focused on the tiny light particles. I saw each one separately as one sees snowflakes drifting separately on a snowy winter day. Each tiny particle of light appeared to be unique and different. I was not fearful for my life. I was calm, and my thoughts were simply *wow, wow,* and *wow!*

When the car landed upright, we managed to crawl out of it even though the top was crushed. We walked away unharmed!

In recent days, I have heard others tell about seeing the same sparkling particles of light in times of crisis. It seems the light particles have the ability to separate into tiny sparkling particles or cluster together, forming an obvious halo or one solid mass of light. I have come to understand that the light particles must be God's angels! Apparently, they come in all shapes and sizes! That is the only explanation I have for what I saw and experienced during the accident! The angels surrounded us that day, as plentiful as feathers in a pillow. They protected us from a wreck that logically should have killed everyone inside the car.

The angel of the Lord encamps around those who fear Him, and rescues them (Psalms 34:7).

Chapter 34

HIS WAYS

God made the heavens, the earth, and the universe. I have no doubt that He spoke light and darkness into existence and created the sun, moon, and stars. It is easy for me to accept the awesome might and power of God with the faith of a child.

However, I suppose the ways of the Lord in the details of life will seem foreign to me as long as I am on this side of Heaven. His concern over the minutiae of life will always amaze and delight me. Why would Almighty God bother Himself with the seemingly trivial or insignificant things—little things, such as an earring?

My husband and I prepared to leave town early one morning. The car was packed, and I had just fastened the clasp on my wristwatch and put on my earrings. I turned to walk out of the bedroom and I heard a quiet voice say, "Go, and look in the mirror." I paused for a moment, questioning why I should receive such instruction, then did as the voice had directed me. I turned on the light and looked closely at myself in the mirror. Then I saw it! One earring was an ordinary white pearl and the other was a silver ball.

With a smile and a bit of wonder I said, "Thank You, Lord."

Would it have mattered if I had worn mismatched earrings? Certainly not. I would have been annoyed by the mistake, but it really would not have mattered in the end. But for some reason, it mattered to the Lord.

That kind of divine intervention is puzzling to me. I am so thankful that God notices everything! I just do not know why He bothers. The fact remains that He does; and I love Him for looking after me.

I remember one summer when everyone in my family had too much going on in their lives. They were always gone from home and I ended up cutting the grass until late one evening. The house was empty and quiet when I finished working in the yard and headed in for a shower. Just as I entered the bedroom, I heard a voice say, "Kneel and pray." I received no instruction as to what I should pray, but I obeyed. I stepped toward the side of the bed and dropped to my knees. I prayed and thanked God for our blessings. I remained there a moment just waiting for further direction, but I heard nothing else.

As I arose from my kneeling position, I turned my head to the left and looked toward the floor. A huge spider scurried off the leg of my jeans and onto the carpet. I killed the spider with my shoe! I remember thanking God for showing me the spider before it bit me or got under the bed! He knew my aversion to spiders, and once again, He was watching over me.

One more story!

One morning, after working in the flower bed on the side of our home, I was alone in the house and walking though the upstairs hall. A voice distinctly said, "Look out the window." I walked to the nearest window and looked out over the flower bed. I admired the freshly cut grass and the shade provided by the two tall hickory trees in the yard; but I was puzzled by that long, straight, black stick near the flower bed. I was sure I had cleaned up all the debris around the flower bed, and the stick should not have been there. At that moment, the long, black stick began to crawl and slither from side to side until it ended up in the flower bed! It was a very long, black snake. I detest snakes and avoid them with great care. When my husband returned home, he searched until he found the snake, then he carried it off by the tail. The snake wasn't poisonous, but it *was* still a snake. Once again, the Lord protected me!

Why would anyone ever doubt God about anything? He is all-powerful, full of love and forgiveness, and He is in charge. He keeps up with the entire universe and still manages to let me know when I am wearing mismatched earrings and warns me about spiders and snakes. He knows the exact number of hairs on my head and knows when a sparrow (or spider) falls.

> *For My thoughts are not your thoughts, nor are your ways My ways," declares the Lord. "For as the heavens are higher than the earth, so are My ways higher than your ways and My thoughts than your thoughts* (Isaiah 55:8-9).

Chapter 35

A DESPERATE PLEA

Cold rain fell on that dark winter evening as the temperature plummeted to 14 degrees. My husband and I felt uneasy when we realized the roads were becoming very slippery. We lived in the country near Mt. Juliet, Tennessee. Our home was quite a ways from downtown Nashville where our son David was attending a night class at Belmont University.

David left the campus at eight o'clock that evening. He drove a new black Mustang, the car of his dreams! It was still an unfamiliar car to him and lightweight. Mustangs were not designed for traveling over icy roads. David had never attempted to drive on ice before; we knew he might be in for some trouble.

Our son began his trip home traveling east on Interstate 40. In a matter of minutes, he realized the Mustang was no match for the present road conditions. I felt helpless each time he called with a progress report. The frozen roads were so treacherous that many cars could not even make it off the exit ramps. David had no choice but to continue eastward. He tried to console me by reminding me what I already knew, "Mom, the Lord is with me!" I knew he was right.

My husband and I prayed together and asked God to send angels to protect David. We prayed for all the motorists who were out that night. Suddenly, I felt the urge to talk to God alone. I went into our bedroom and closed the door. I prayed, "Lord, You can do anything! Will You just melt the ice before him and bring David home safely tonight, please?"

When I arose, the fear was gone, and I had a certain knowledge that David should detour from his planned route. I had an inner peace that he should make his way toward Andrew Jackson Parkway! It was unlikely that road would be salted, but I knew what God imparted when I prayed.

David agreed to change his course as soon as he was able and I felt a sense of relief! From that moment on, Burke and I knew what we needed to do. We prepared the four-wheel-drive SUV for any foreseeable difficulties we might encounter and drove toward David with great caution. We saw many cars in ditches, yet we moved slowly but surely along at a snail's pace.

We were pleasantly surprised when our son called to say he had managed to reach the hardware store in Hermitage. He said, "This is as far as I go! My car is in one piece, and I am going to park it here!"

When we arrived, David was happy to see us! The first thing he said was, "Man oh man! What a trip! I was glad to see the ice melted on Andrew Jackson Parkway! I was the only car in sight, and I drove at normal speed. Water sprayed up from my tires as I drove!"

We traveled home the same way we came, very slowly and on ice. We all knew it was not possible for ice to melt when the temperature was 14 degrees. It was not humanly possible for our son to drive at normal speed with water splashing on the side of his car! That night, we received a reminder, "...*With God all things are possible*" (Matt. 19:26).

I believe a merciful Heavenly Father heard a desperate mother's childlike plea for her faithful son. He answered her prayer by sending just what she asked for and God received the glory. God still receives the glory today each time the story is told!

The situation required assistance that only God could provide! Our family made it home safely and we arrived in our warm, country kitchen where the embers glowed in the fireplace, inviting us to warm our cold hands. It was so good to be home; our family was safe and under one roof! God's divine intervention demonstrated His real presence. Prayers of praise and thanksgiving overflowed from our hearts as we drifted off to sleep with the assurance that we were surely loved and safe in our Heavenly Father's care.

> *He* [God] *sends forth His command to the earth; His word runs very swiftly. He gives snow like wool; He scatters the frost like ashes. He casts forth His ice as fragments; who can stand before His cold? He sends forth His word and melts them* [the ice]; *He causes His wind to blow and the waters to flow* (Psalms 147:15-18).

Chapter 36

VOICE OF A FRIEND

Summer was Annie Scheele's favorite time of year. The Atlantic shore beckoned, and Annie often took her daughter, Leila, to enjoy the golden warmth of the beach near their Rockville, Maryland, home. Annie was thrilled each time she watched three-year-old Leila's eyes light up with excitement as they walked across the beautiful expanse of sparkling sand to the water's edge.

Louis, the 17-year-old brother of Annie's childhood friend, often joined Annie and Leila on the beach that summer. Louis and Leila had formed a grand friendship. They took long walks together, waves lapping at their feet as they searched for seashells to add to Leila's growing collection. Leila adored Louis, and he seemed to enjoy his time with the little girl. He became a welcome addition to their beach outings. Louis was an all-around good kid.

Annie was sure the summer of 1977 was one she would long remember.

Several months later, the bitter winds of winter descended. One particularly cold December night, Louis left a party and sat in his car as the engine idled. Unaware of the deadly carbon monoxide fumes that seeped into the vehicle, Louis soon lost consciousness. Louis' young life was cut short; he died that frozen, winter night from accidental carbon monoxide poisoning. His premature death was a tragic ending to a life that offered so much promise.

A short time after Louis died, Leila rode in the back seat of the car as Annie navigated heavy traffic on Piercefield Road. Annie's day had been stressful and she was not nearly as focused on driving as she should have been. With her mind on other matters, Annie was oblivious to the congested intersection just ahead of her. Suddenly, she felt a strong hand grab her shoulder and she clearly heard Louis yell, "Annie, red light!" Without hesitation, she responded to the voice; she hit the brakes, bringing the car to a sudden stop just short of the busy intersection. An inevitable accident had been avoided. Had she not stopped when she did, she and Leila could have been severely injured, maybe even killed.

Thoughts raced through Annie's mind! From the back seat, Leila said, "Mommy, Louis is with us, and he told you to stop, didn't he?" It was a profound moment. Louis was certainly dead. Yet, Annie could still feel his hand as he grabbed her shoulder; she could still hear his voice as he yelled the warning that saved their lives. Louis had been with them in the car, and she and Leila both heard him!

Annie cannot explain her after-death encounter with Louis; but she firmly believes no explanation is necessary. Her faith was challenged, encouraged, and strengthened by the experience; and she has gained a certain and sure peace. Annie says she is keenly aware that the body is just a shell for something much greater than this temporary life; it is the container for the eternal soul.

Though the events may be beyond rationalization, Annie remains convinced that something miraculous and incredible occurred that day on Piercefield Road.

Chapter 37

ANGEL FOOD

Burke Aldridge grimaced from the pain of lung and bone cancer; he slowly opened his eyes as he tried to make sense of regaining consciousness on day 21 of hospitalization. His eyes surveyed the small hospital room. He was uncertain of his surroundings. I gently explained to Burke, telling him he had been moved from the Intensive Care Unit back to the Critical Care Unit at Baptist Hospital in Nashville. The room in CCU provided less human interference from medical personnel and more privacy for Burke and our family.

Burke had not eaten in two weeks; on the last Sunday afternoon of his life, he announced, "I want something to eat!" Our son was present and exclaimed to his dad that he would go anywhere and find anything he desired. Burke said, "I only want a bite of something...I wish I had a bite of a Snickers® candy bar and a bite of cantaloupe." The Lord provided for Burke that day by undeniable godly and divine intervention.

One bite of a Snickers® candy bar and one bite of cantaloupe was Burke's last earthly meal. He wanted no more and no less. Earlier that same day, our daughter, Donna, came to the hospital to see her dad and she brought fresh fruit for me to eat, which I didn't eat. Fresh cantaloupe in a small, sealed container sat on a shelf by the sink; it took only seconds to grant half of Burke's request!

My childhood friend, Mildred Barrett, traveled 350 miles the day before to see Burke and brought a bag of snacks for me. I didn't know what the entire bag contained; however, I caught a glimpse of the word Snickers® when I moved the bag from ICU to CCU the day before. Sure enough, the bag rendered a package of bite-size Snickers® candy bars! Burke's wish came true in less than a minute!

I did not think it was strange that God supplied Burke's last meal before we or he knew he wanted it. It was merely evidence of God's personal touch! During those moments while David and I shared the food with Burke, I felt surrounded by the merciful and loving presence of an awesome God. I knew without question God was with us!

To this day, when I think of cantaloupe and Snickers® candy bars, I think of "angel food"! God provided angel food for Burke that cold February day, and I gratefully and publicly acknowledge His marvelous divine intervention!

> *Are not two sparrows sold for a cent? And yet not one of them will fall to the ground apart from your Father. But the very hairs of your head are all numbered. So do not fear; you are more valuable than many sparrows. Therefore everyone who confesses Me before men, I will also confess him before My Father who is in heaven. But whoever denies Me before men, I will also deny him before My Father who is in heaven* (Matthew 10:29-33).

Chapter 38

A Message of Hope

Laura[1] grew up in the Church of Christ. She knew about Jesus and had often heard the message of salvation. However, Laura spent most of her life running from God, refusing to accept His free gift of new, abundant life through His Son.

Determined to live her life according to her own rules, Laura ran headlong into a lifestyle of self-destruction. She became a drug user and, ultimately, a drug addict. When her funds were exhausted, Laura became a prostitute to fund her habit. Tomorrow was never on Laura's radar; she spent her days in efforts to feed her growing addiction.

Circumstances intervened in Laura's wasted life when she learned she was dying of cancer. Impending death cast a shocking clarity to her shattered life and meaningless existence. Laura was filled with shame and regret. She began to realize her need for God. Laura's bruised and hardened heart became more tender and open; she was ready to accept God's salvation—she was ready to follow Jesus.

Laura's doctor admitted her to Baptist Hospital for treatment to prolong her life. Chaplain Lewis Lamberth visited her often during her stay. He spent time getting to know her and telling her about Jesus. He explained to her how Jesus died on the cross for each of us so our sins would be forgiven; he told her the blood of Jesus covers all sin. Understanding began to dawn on Laura; God's truth became a beacon of hope.

Finally, Laura prayed a simple but heartfelt prayer. She asked God for forgiveness and accepted Jesus as her Savior and Lord.

After Laura committed her life to Jesus, she wanted to do all her newfound Lord required. Having never been baptized, Laura felt a strong need to do so. She wanted to make a statement about her decision to follow the Lord and to confirm her new life in God. Chaplain Lamberth was more than thrilled to comply with her wishes.

Soon after her baptism, Laura left the hospital with a new hope in spite of her dire prognosis. She lived for only a few more months before returning to Baptist Hospital to die.

After Laura's death, her sister-in-law contacted Chaplain Lamberth and told him an interesting story. She and her husband were lying in bed asleep on the night of Laura's death. It was about ten o'clock in the evening when she awoke to see Laura standing near the foot of the bed. She looked 20 years younger than her actual age and she was dressed in white clothing. Laura said, "I'm okay, don't worry!" She said nothing further before she faded out of sight. Laura's sister-in-law immediately phoned the hospital. The nurse informed her that Laura died only minutes before.

Laura's sister-in-law knew Chaplain Lamberth was instrumental in Laura's conversion. She believed Laura wanted him to know that she had indeed made it to the other side and was in Heaven, doing just fine!

Chaplain Lewis Lamberth Jr. is still doing God's work. Today he is the Director of Pastoral Care at Baptist Hospital in Nashville, Tennessee.

NOTE

1. A fictitious name was used to protect the identity of the deceased.

Chapter 39

A SERVANT'S HEART

A sense of freedom and purpose stirred in Jaimee Underwood as she traveled toward Knoxville, just east of Nashville, Tennessee, on Interstate 40. She was a single mother of two small children and a successful criminal defense attorney living in Franklin, Tennessee. Jaimee was a strong-willed woman who recently survived a painful divorce and premature death of her father whom she dearly loved. She went through some tough emotional times, but with much determination she seemed to be getting her life back on track.

Instinctively, Jaimee focused on the positive, looking forward to a great weekend. Her thoughts drifted toward the anticipated reunion with her six-year-old daughter, Alexa, and her two-year-old son, Lawson. They had spent a week with their dad and Jaimee was anxious to see them.

The date was July 19, 2004, and the time was approximately 6:30 in the evening. Jaimee was driving in the far left lane of four eastbound lanes of traffic when she ran over a small object that punctured her tire; she pulled the huge SUV to the left shoulder of the road into an extremely narrow space between the heavy traffic and a large, concrete barrier. The flat tire was on the passenger's side, nearest the oncoming traffic. Jaimee realized the danger of her situation. She reported her predicament to her motor club and contacted the Tennessee Highway Patrol for assistance.

Police officer Christy Dedman responded to the call. She pulled her patrol car close behind Jaimee's vehicle and activated the emergency lights of the cruiser. Everything was by the book—the scene was a textbook example of safe procedure employed in an effort to divert traffic around the disabled SUV long enough for Jaimee to change the tire.

Jaimee looked into the smiling face of Officer Christy Dedman, and they both tried to remain calm in the face of their precarious dilemma. Seconds later, Jaimee found herself lying flat on her back, dazed, confused, and in excruciating pain. An eastbound tractor-trailer rig, traveling at approximately 70 miles per hour, crashed into the back of the patrol car, which in turn crashed into Jaimee and Officer Dedman.

A 250-pound piece of the demolished police car pinned Jaimee against the pavement. Her breathing was limited and her pain was indescribable.

An off-duty truck driver came to Jaimee's aid. He knelt down beside her and noticed she appeared to be unconscious; however, her eyes were open. Small pieces of crushed glass filled her motionless eyes. He could not believe she was alive. The stranger gently picked the glass out of Jaimee's eyes with his fingertips.

An off-duty paramedic emerged from one of the cars in the traffic that backed up for several miles due to the accident. Jaimee feared she was dying, but the paramedic assured her she would be all right; the expression on his face said otherwise. Jaimee began praying she would live long enough to say goodbye to her children and family. The paramedic stayed with Jaimee until help arrived, holding her head so she could not see the body of Christy Dedman lying motionless beside her. The impact of the crash killed Officer Christy Dedman instantly.

An ambulance arrived and transported Jaimee to the trauma ward at Vanderbilt Medical Center in Nashville. She was critically injured and losing blood at an alarming rate; however, she remained awake and aware during the entire ordeal, resisting the ever-present urge to allow darkness and oblivion to render her unconscious.

Jaimee sustained a traumatic brain injury, lacerations to her spleen, liver, and kidney, and an "open-book" pelvic fracture that shattered her pelvic bone into three pieces. The internal bleeding was profuse, requiring numerous blood transfusions. Jaimee's pelvic fracture necessitated surgery. Large screws and metal rods affixed to her pelvic bone literally held her together. After suffering a collapsed lung on two separate occasions, Jaimee's condition stabilized.

One of Jaimee's nurses was exceptionally kind; she went beyond the call of duty to be helpful. One morning shortly after the accident, the nurse shared an extraordinary account with Jaimee. "When I was with you in your room last night, I felt Christy Dedman's presence very strongly. I finished cleaning you up, and I went to the sink to wash my hands. When I looked in the mirror, I saw Officer Christy Dedman standing behind me. She was standing there, smiling at you! She was dressed in her uniform and hat." The nurse told Jaimee, "When I turned from the mirror, Christy vanished."

Jaimee's nurse reported seeing Officer Dedman in Jaimee's room on several occasions over the next few days. Christy appeared calm, and she smiled whenever she appeared. Each time, Christy vanished when the nurse turned to look directly at her.

Morphine, a strong painkiller, was used to control Jaimee's relentless pain, leaving her thinking somewhat impaired. Jaimee wondered if her impaired thinking was the reason Christy appeared to the nurse instead of her.

To make matters worse, Jaimee suffered terribly from survivor's guilt; she was emotionally devastated. She could not understand why God spared her life and not Christy's. Jaimee's grief was tremendous and she felt responsible for Christy's death because Christy died helping her.

Christy's after-death appearances offered comfort to Jaimee and Christy's family. The appearances helped Jaimee understand that Christy did not blame her, and that Christy forgave her! Jaimee was able to deal with her grief over Christy by knowing she was still very much alive and in a far better place.

Jaimee's recovery did not happen overnight, but she did recover. Jaimee said, "The experience was a powerful thing that changed my life. Before the accident, I acknowledged God; however, I did not appreciate or serve God. I have come to a point in my life where I have truly accepted Jesus as my personal Savior. I accepted Jesus and received baptism at the age of fourteen, but I drifted away from my spiritual life. The wreck was a turning point. Because of all that happened to me, I have reconnected with Jesus in a profound way! I 'get it' now!"

Jaimee attends regular worship services and believes she is a better mom, a better lawyer, and a stronger Christian because of the adversities she has faced in her life.

> Officer Christy Dedman died at the age of 35, leaving behind her parents, a brother, aunts, uncles, cousins, and many friends. She was the second female police officer to be killed in the line of duty in Nashville. The Nashville Police Department posthumously awarded Officer Dedman the highest Medal of Honor bestowed by the Nashville Police Department—the Medal of Valor. Today a simple cross on Interstate 40, just east of Nashville, marks the place where Christy's life in this world ended tragically.

Chapter 40

WHITE FEATHERS

I hugged my 16-year-old grandson just before he left the church and handed him a BP gas card. Jacob owned his very first car and had been driving for less than a week. He grinned and thanked me. Jacob kissed me on the cheek before he drove away that morning on his way to see his girlfriend.

After attending early service, I went into my Sunday school room for class. After class, a young woman ran to me and said, "Jacob has been in an accident! Have you heard?" My heart skipped a beat, and I ran to my car to find my phone!

I learned that Jacob was traveling on an unfamiliar road in search of a BP gas station when the accident occurred. Jacob in his car and a woman in her car both arrived at an intersection at precisely the same moment. They were traveling at speeds of approximately 45 miles per hour when they crashed. Both vehicles were instantly totaled! Each car contained one occupant, the driver. Only by God's grace, each driver walked away from the accident without a scratch.

Jacob's mom, Donna, arrived at the scene of the accident shortly after it happened. My daughter hugged her son and looked him over, making certain he was all right. She looked at Jacob's demolished Volvo in horror. The safety airbag deployed on impact.

My grandson said, "Mom, I never knew airbags were filled with feathers!"

Donna replied, "There are no feathers in airbags! They are filled with air. Why do you think they are filled with feathers?"

"When I crashed, I saw white feathers all around me! White feathers were flying everywhere and were all over the seat!" Jacob exclaimed.

Donna said the peace of God, which surpasses all comprehension, filled her at that moment.

> *And the peace of God, which surpasses all comprehension, will guard your hearts and your minds in Christ Jesus* (Philippians 4:7).

Donna explained to Jacob, "Since you started driving, I having been praying for God to keep you safe, and each day I plead the blood of Jesus over you—and I claim the 91st Psalm over you!"

> *He who dwells in the secret place of the Most High shall abide under the shadow of the Almighty. I will say of the Lord, "He is my refuge and my fortress; my God, in Him I will trust!" ...He shall cover you with His feathers, and under His wings you shall take refuge.... For He shall give His angels charge over you, to keep* [guard] *you in all your ways* (Psalms 91:1-2,4,11 NKJV).

Jacob jokingly but truthfully remarked, "So angels really do have feathers! White feathers!" Jacob was amazed when he realized God's hand of protection had surely saved him and the other driver! *The presence of the white feathers seemed to stress the fact that God wanted Jacob to remember who saved him!*

Upon further inspection of the car, Jacob's mom noticed a small crushed section in the lower passenger side of the windshield. It appeared that a passenger's head had landed there, except for the fact there was no passenger! Jacob and our family believe an angel was riding with him at the time of the crash, and for that we are forever grateful to God!

Chapter 41

I'll Fly Away

I met Debbie Matthews, a music executive, one cold, gray November morning. A fine and foggy mist filled the air. My Monday required some rearranging because of an appointment cancellation. I thought of a music business matter I could handle, considering the fact that I suddenly had a free morning. I experienced a holy prompting to go at once! I went online, seeking the address for a publishing company, then drove toward Nashville with directions on the seat beside me. I headed for 25 Music Square East on Music Row.

Parking places on Music Row are nearly nonexistent, so I decided to find the building then park somewhere in the area and walk back to the business. I located 23 Music Square East but did not see 25 Music Square East. I circled the block a second time; I still did not see the number 25, and no parking space was in sight. I circled the third time and discovered a vacant parking space at the end of a row of parallel-parked cars at 23 Music Square East. I claimed that spot at once and noticed a woman four cars ahead of me, standing outside her car. She appeared to be looking for something.

I approached the woman and made an inquiry about the missing street number, and she smiled and said, "That business has moved. If you will come inside with me, I will help you find the new address." We entered her business called Valhalla Music Group. We exchanged introductions and business cards. She looked at my card and she asked me several questions. When she realized I write about people who have experienced divine intervention in their lives, she said, "I think maybe the Lord sent you to me today!"

Debbie went on to tell me it was her first day back at work after a six-month break. She took the time off to run for a Senate seat. Her run was unsuccessful, and her faith was sorely tested during those months. She was weary from the good, the bad, and the ugly things she encountered in the field of politics. She needed to be reminded that God was real and still in control.

Debbie said, "When I drove into Nashville this morning, I parked outside this building in the very spot where you are now parked. Something told me 'not yet.' I pulled away from the curb and circled the building. When I approached the building the second time, I passed up your parking spot and parked where you found me, then I could not find my keys. I saw the keys as soon as you said, 'Pardon me.'"

I laughed and said to Debbie, "God more than likely caused you to do that because He knows I can't parallel park!" I said jokingly, "My insurance company forbids me to do that ever again! God must have hidden your keys until I reached you."

God's timing never ceases to amaze me! God had her park there and save the spot for me then move out of the spot at precisely the right moment so I could park there. God spoke to Debbie and to me that day; we both heard Him and obeyed Him!

We laughed, yet both of us knew our meeting was not by chance! Holy manipulation orchestrated our meeting! I ventured out and asked, "Do you perhaps have a story for my next book?" Debbie smiled and nodded yes. She shared with me the story about her mother's death. Sometimes, the way I get my stories is almost as amazing as the stories!

Debbie's mother, Beverly Jean Chapman, died from oat cell carcinoma of the lungs. She died 15 months after she learned she had cancer.

Beverly's nickname was "Jackie." She was a beautiful person and an elegant woman. Jackie's eyes were green, and her smile was contagious; she never met a stranger. Everyone who knew her loved her. Debbie loved her mom very much.

Early in the morning on the day of Beverly's death, Debbie left her home in Columbia, Tennessee, to have her hair cut. She left her mom at her home under the care of a hospice nurse. Later that morning, Debbie received a call to return home; her mom's death appeared imminent.

Debbie returned home as fast as she could! Many visitors and a minister surrounded her mom, so Debbie asked them to leave the room; she wanted the death experience to be a personal and private matter. Debbie's husband, Jason, and one hospice nurse remained in the room. She asked her singer/songwriter husband to sing, but he couldn't because of the tears. Jason loved his mother-in-law very much; sadness overwhelmed him.

Debbie quickly found a CD and pressed play. The voice of Vern Gosden singing "I'll Fly Away" filled the room with song and praises in a final farewell to Beverly. Everyone joined in and started singing the song! Debbie contemplated the suffering she saw in her mom with lung cancer; then she visualized the heavenly realm she was about to enter. Debbie looked into her mom's beautiful jade green eyes as her mom looked back at her. Her mom communicated without speaking a word. Words poured from Debbie's spirit through her mouth as she affectionately cried out to her mother, "Run, Jackie, run!"

At that moment, Debbie saw with her eyes her mom's spirit actually leaving her body. A white mist, a white sweeping vapor, soared from her body then swirled upward and away from her motionless body. The spirit appeared to be running! Debbie never questioned the experience; she felt great comfort from what she saw. There was no fear! She knew her devout Christian mother was now completely healed and Heaven bound!

...He will dwell among them, and they shall be His people, and God Himself will be among them, and He will wipe away every tear from their eyes; and there will no longer be any death; there will no longer be any mourning, or crying, or pain; the first things have passed away (Revelation 21:3-4).

Chapter 42

MEGAN'S STORY

For the first five years of Megan Welch's life, she and her parents lived next door to her mother's parents in a home near Little Rock, Arkansas. Those times would live forever in Megan's mind because her Papa was her favorite person in the whole world! He laughed a lot, had a quick wit and always had a twinkle in his eye! Megan was the apple of her Papa's eye. Papa, Harry Charter, was a retired military man having served in the Air Force for twenty years. He retired in 1976 then spent much of his time with family and playing golf with his friends.

When she was pre-school age, Megan did not attend a daycare facility nor did she require a sitter. She stayed in the home of her care-giving grandparents on a regular basis. As a small child, when Megan got into trouble with her parents, she often ran into the back yard in search of Papa. She knew without question he would come to her aid, reaching out and lifting her over the fence where he would console her with kind words and adoring hugs and kisses. Megan loved her Granny and the rest of her family but no one could compare to her beloved Papa!

Megan's parents divorced before she turned six years old and that serious life change caused her to cling to her Papa even more than before. He was a constant in her life, one she could count on without fail. When Megan entered the sixth grade in 2003, she did so in Dallas, Texas. She felt like she was a long way from home but she adapted and managed well.

On May 8, 2004, Megan returned to her home from the park down the street. As soon as she walked into the house, she received the news. Life as Megan knew it, ended that day and would never be the same again.

Megan learned her grandfather had suffered a fatal heart attack on his way home from the golf course. He died suddenly. When Megan heard the news, she collapsed onto the floor sobbing uncontrollably. Heartbroken and in disbelief, she accepted the devastating truth as well as she could. She had never known pain of that magnitude and the separation was nearly too much to bear. Megan had no choice but to endure the loss.

Months turned into years but time did not heal the heartache as others told her it would. Dreams in the nighttime haunted Megan and reminded her of the void in her life without her grandfather. Numerous times, she awoke crying in the hours before dawn.

In the summer time of 2009, Megan went to visit her Uncle Kenny and Aunt Pam who lived a couple of hours away from Little Rock. Her dad had returned there from Switzerland. She was a young woman by then, eighteen years old, still scarred by the heartsick emotions in the absence of the one she loved the most. Megan and her step mom, Vicki, shared the guest bedroom the first night.

Megan experienced a vivid dream that night. She saw herself as a tiny girl again, sitting in the lap of her grandfather. Repeatedly, in the dream, Megan spoke to her Papa pleading with him, saying, "I never want to see you go away again! I don't want to let go!" The loud sobbing awoke Vicki who then told Megan she should pray for a sign from God, to comfort her and to reassure her that her Papa was all right and with God. Megan took Vicki's advice and prayed herself back to sleep.

The following evening after dinner, Megan received a phone call from a number she did not recognize. She was eating when the call came in so she allowed the call to go to voice mail. Minutes later, she stepped outside to listen to the message that startled her and amazed her!

The message was a thirty-second segment of a song about angels. Megan heard music and the lyrics *'Angels, answer me, are you near if rain should fall?"* The song was unfamiliar to Megan. Vicki was not certain but believed the vocalist sounded like Enya so Megan searched online for 'angel lyrics'. Quickly she discovered the song on the voice mail was the song called 'Angeles' performed by Enya. Megan tried to call the number on her phone only to discover the number was not in service. She thought, "That is impossible!"

Megan certainly received the song about angels but she was puzzled about how she received the song. It was impossible for a call to originate from a disconnected number. Slowly but surely, through the tears, Megan understood she had received a message from heaven. The comprehension was enormous because God had answered Megan's prayer, sending her a sign like the one she asked for. Finally, Megan understood her Papa was in Heaven with God and the angels; he was perfectly fine! She knew she would see him again. An amazing peace settled over Megan as she realized God was listening and watching over her. He heard her prayer and He answered her prayer with the sign she needed so desperately.

Megan Welch's faith grew stronger and stronger because of her trials and the time God evidenced Himself to her when she needed Him most. She presently attends school at a university in Texas. She plans to teach when she graduates in the spring of 2013.

Megan said, "I know God was listening that night, He knew I needed Him in that moment. He is always listening! The incident affected me in a powerful way, making me a stronger woman with stronger faith in Jesus Christ."

> *Behold, I am the Lord, the God of all flesh; is anything too difficult for Me?* (Jeremiah 32:27)

Chapter 42

MIRACULOUS TRILOGY

PART 1

Although the Vietnam War still raged abroad, Danny Kellum enlisted in the Army immediately after he graduated from college. Soon after completing officer candidate school, he was ordered to active duty in Vietnam. Danny was a newlywed and struggled to tell his young wife he would soon be leaving. His wife feared he would die in combat, but Danny was committed and courageous. He came from a long line of patriots; he was ready to serve his country, no matter the cost.

Danny's company was deployed. Danny served as a forward observer for the 101st Airborne division, assigned to Alpha Company, the second of the 502nd Infantry. Their mission was "search and destroy." This meant they were sent into a particular area by helicopter with orders to destroy the enemy before the enemy destroyed them. Fear and anxiety were constant companions for Alpha Company and its forward observer.

With incredible clarity, Danny recalls a particular mission. Alpha Company had been in the same location for ten days, a strange departure from protocol, which required relocation every 24 hours. Danny remembers, "We were in the mountainous jungles of South Vietnam securing a location that overlooked the Song Bo River. During that time, we were interdicting enemy concentration in the area. Through intercepted enemy communication, we discovered that our position was going to be overrun by the enemy that night." Alpha Company would have to move out.

Believing there were enemy soldiers just outside the area, Danny's platoon waited for darkness to begin the search for a safe place to spend the night. No flashlights aided their search; they navigated through the black night with only the guide of a compass. Unable to locate an elevated place where gravity would make defense easier (it is a much simpler task to throw hand grenades downhill), they took refuge in a low-lying area.

Later that evening, an artillery barrage was mounted against the recently vacated location, now overrun by the enemy. The night was pitch black, making accurate targeting of the area nearly impossible. In an effort to direct the artillery, a smoke round from World War II was fired into the air above the vicinity of the enemy's location. Both rounds failed to explode and crashed to the earth. Although Danny could not see the smoke, he heard the round's impact. Using the sound as his guide, Danny fired two rounds of high explosives toward the target. One round went off unexpectedly close. The explosion was only a few feet away from where Danny and his troops were located; however, Danny and his troops were totally unscathed.

Danny says, "I still don't know what happened that night, but that round almost killed us." As Danny relates the circumstances of his brush with death, it is obvious he is convinced that divine intervention saved his life.

Part 2

Two days later, Danny's platoon had made its way to a clearing atop a hill, a makeshift landing zone for helicopters. From that position, Danny began to shoot artillery toward the enemy's location.

"As I stood there, I heard a piece of shrapnel coming at us," said Danny. "A bullet makes a whistling sound; shrapnel makes a chirping sound. You can't see shrapnel coming any more than you can see a bullet coming at you; they move at the same speed. It was singing through the air. I decided to stand very still and let it miss me. It did not miss me. It hit me in the heart area of my chest! I was knocked on the ground. It cut and bruised me, but it didn't kill me."

Later Danny held the piece of shrapnel up against his chest and had his radiotelephone operator take a picture. The shrapnel was almost five inches long and nearly two inches wide, a jagged hunk of metal that looked like it was ripped from a solid sheet of steel. Mistakenly, the roll of film containing the photo was sent to his wife. She wrote Danny asking what that was in his hand against his chest. He neglected to answer her question in his next letter. Only when he was safely home did he tell her the real story about how God saved him from certain death!

Danny now recalls, "If that piece of shrapnel had been turned another fraction of an inch, or had I moved another fraction of an inch, if I had tried to dodge a fraction of an inch, it would have gone through me and taken out my heart and lungs instantly!

"I reached down and picked it up, then got down on my knees and thanked God for sparing my life. As a believer, I knew that I was alive because God Himself had protected me; He had positioned me perfectly still. Then He positioned that piece of shrapnel in such a way that it broadsided me instead of slicing through me." Danny has never doubted that, once again, divine intervention protected him from death.

PART 3

It has been about 40 years since Danny Kellum began his tour of duty in the Army. Second Lieutenant Danny Kellum is now Dr. Kellum. He served as the headmaster of Donelson Christian Academy, a private Christian school in Nashville, Tennessee, for many years.

His present lifestyle is much different from the life-threatening conditions of an artillery forward observer. God's protective love is still active in Dr. Kellum's life; divine intervention is still a fact in this grateful man's experience.

A few years ago, Dr. Kellum was assisting in the disassembly of a large scaffold that had been used during graduation to hold a huge drapery. One piece of scaffolding had been disengaged and lowered to the ground. Dr. Kellum worked to loosen the next section. Suddenly, he lost his footing and fell 24 feet to the gymnasium floor! His body struck the scaffolding many times before he landed heavily, his back and head crashing with great force into the solid, wooden surface.

Dr. Kellum remained conscious after the fall. He even remembers hearing a student call 911 for assistance. He was taken by ambulance to the emergency room of Vanderbilt Medical Center. Dr. Kellum was thoroughly examined due to the distance and impact of his fall. A number of scrapes and bruises were found, but Dr. Kellum had miraculously escaped any serious injury. He walked out of the emergency room that same day!

"It was a miraculous event from God," said Dr. Kellum. His life had been spared once again.

EPILOGUE

Dr. Kellum is able to look back over many, many years with genuine gratitude toward God, still giving Him all the glory for each time his life has been spared.

Dr. Kellum has a daughter, Deeannah, and two sons, Dan and Rob. Both of his sons have served in the U.S. Military. The advice Dr. Kellum offered his sons before they deployed was this: "Be faithful and true to God. Make sure you share your faith with others. There will always be people who are looking and searching for answers to life and life's questions; Jesus is the answer. Others need to hear your testimony to be able to fully understand your relationship to God. Do not think people will observe your lives and see Jesus. You must share the Gospel."

Prayer of Salvation

If you do not know Jesus Christ, here is an idea of what you might want to pray to God. It is a personal request from you to God.

If you confess with your mouth, "Jesus is Lord," and believe in your heart that God raised Him from the dead, you will be saved (Romans 10:9 NIV).

Dear God,

I know I have broken Your laws and my sins have separated me from You. I am sorry and I now repent (turn away from) my past sinful life toward You. Please forgive me and keep me from sinning again. I believe Your Son Jesus Christ died on the cross for my sins and He was raised from the dead and He is alive today. I invite Jesus into my heart as my Lord and Savior. Please change my heart, dear Lord, and make me be like You. I love You and thank You.

In Jesus' name, I pray. Amen.

ABOUT FAYE ALDRIDGE

Faye Aldridge is the author of two previous books about miraculous occurrences. She wrote *A Fax from Heaven* and *Real Messages from Heaven*. Both books offer undeniable proof of God's intervention in our lives and proof of life after death. Her current book, *Evidence of His Presence*, is a collaboration of true stories about Divine intervention, angels, and near-death and after-death experiences. Her books are reminders of the reality of God, Heaven, and hell and that the cross of Jesus Christ is the only bridge to Heaven.

A NOTE FROM FAYE ALDRIDGE

I am very interested in hearing from readers who would care to share their near-death experiences, after-death appearances, or messages, angel encounters, miraculous answers to prayer, and stories of divine intervention. Please visit my website at www.realmessagesfromheaven. com. If I am able to use your story in a future book, I will contact you for permission.

Faye Aldridge

DESTINY IMAGE PUBLISHERS, INC.

"Promoting Inspired Lives."

VISIT OUR NEW SITE HOME AT
WWW.DESTINYIMAGE.COM

FREE SUBSCRIPTION TO DI NEWSLETTER

Receive free unpublished articles by top DI authors, exclusive

discounts, and free downloads from our best and newest books.

Visit www.destinyimage.com to subscribe.

Write to: Destiny Image
               P.O. Box 310
               Shippensburg, PA 17257-0310

Call: 1-800-722-6774

Email: orders@destinyimage.com

For a complete list of our titles or to place an order
online, visit www.destinyimage.com.

FIND US ON FACEBOOK OR FOLLOW US ON TWITTER.

www.facebook.com/destinyimage
www.twitter.com/destinyimage